OPEN UNIVERSITY PRESS
Gender and Education Series
Editors
ROSEMARY DEEM
Professor of Educational Research, University of Lancaster
GABY WEINER
Principal Lecturer in Education at South Bank University

The series provides compact and clear accounts of relevant research and practice in the field of gender and education. It is aimed at trainee and practising teachers, and parents and others with an educational interest in ending gender inequality. All age-ranges will be included, and there will be an emphasis on ethnicity as well as gender. Series authors are all established educational practitioners or researchers.

Shaping Up to Womanhood

GENDER AND GIRLS' PHYSICAL EDUCATION

Sheila Scraton

Open University Press
Buckingham • Philadelphia

Open University Press
Celtic Court
22 Ballmoor
Buckingham
MK 18 1XW

and
1900 Frost Road, Suite 101
Bristol, PA 19007, USA

First Published 1992

A catalogue record of this book is available from the British Library

Library of Congress Cataloging-in-Publication Data

Scraton, Sheila. 1950-
    Shaping up to womanhood : gender and girls' physical education /
by Sheila Scraton.
        p. cm. — (Gender and education series)
    Includes bibliographical references (p.) and index.
    ISBN 0-335-09693-X
    1. Physical education for women.   2. Sexism in education.
3. Feminist theory.   I. Title.   II. Series.
GV439.S43 1992
613.7′045—dc20
                                                            92-8264
                                                               CIP

Typeset by Colset Pte Ltd, Singapore
Printed in Great Britain by J.W. Arrowsmith Ltd, Bristol

Contents

Series Editor's Introduction

It is particularly pleasing to be able to write the series editor's introduction to this book because I supervised Sheila Scraton's PhD, the work on which this book is based. We have largely avoided publishing books in the series which are taken from PhD theses, because we want to give teachers themselves, rather than academics, the chance to write for their peers. However, in this case Sheila Scraton both has the necessary practitioner background and, in our view, has something of central importance to say to all teachers, whatever their subject specialism or sector. When Sheila began the research which is central to the focus of the book, in the early 1980s, there was already a great deal of research on gender differentiation in many aspects of the secondary school curriculum. But none of this (in the UK context) touched upon or considered physical education (PE), which, despite the 1975 Sex Discrimination Act, has remained one of the most gender-segregated aspects of the secondary curriculum in England and Wales. Sheila, as a former PE teacher herself, was uniquely placed to study this issue. Her research is important for many reasons. She provides an original, sensitive, well-observed and detailed comparison of the teaching of PE to girls in a number of different contexts. There is a crucial consideration of the relationship between sexuality and the body, an area beginning to be of wider feminist interest, and physical activity. An excellent set of practical recommendations for PE teachers is provided, which should offer the PE profession much food for thought. The book dispels the myth that sport and leisure should not be the concern of feminists and promotes instead the view that physical activity is very important to adolescent girls. Sheila Scraton does not content herself, as many would, with merely critiquing what happens now in schools; she offers positive alternatives. The messages that are transmitted by the book are of value to all of us who work in education, whether in nursery, primary, secondary, further, adult or higher education. Unless girls and women are encouraged to think positively about their bodies, their sexuality and the significance of physical activity to their well-being and capacity to assert themselves in any situation or environment in which they find themselves, then a major potential vehicle through which women's oppression by men can be reduced, will have been lost. We hope that by reading this book, many more teachers will realize that PE is not just a marginal school subject which gets in the way of more academic subjects and is also hated by girls themselves, but an area of the curriculum which is just as important as English or Maths and deserves as much attention.

Rosemary Deem

Acknowledgements

There are many people who have given me support, encouragement and critical comment both during my research and in the preparation of this book. Although I cannot thank them all individually their help has been invaluable. I would like to give special thanks to Rosemary Deem for her help, encouragement and supervision; Eileen Bragg, Sally Channon and Barney Brown for the typing and production of the original thesis and this manuscript; Pat Craddock, Deena Haydon, Chris Hughes and Sue Hughes for their personal and intellectual support; Leeds Polytechnic and all my colleagues for time, encouragement and friendship; the staff and pupils of the local education authority who allowed me into their schools to carry out my research and who made me feel welcome. Finally I thank Paul and Sean Scraton for their love and Phil Scraton for his continuous unselfish love, support, advice and commitment in every aspect of my academic and personal life.

Introduction

The research context

The 'equality' debate has been a central issue in the politics of education and schooling since the 1944 Education Act. Initially the debate focused on the relationship between social class and educational achievement, emphasizing the need for programmes of 'compensatory education'. However, the recognition that in practice these policy reforms were having little meaningful effect on class-linked achievement encouraged a 'new sociology of education' emphasizing wider issues of class relations in British society and examining the relationship between class, the curriculum and 'legitimate' knowledge (Young 1971). This work laid the foundations for the development of critical perspectives which argued for the recognition of structural relationships between schooling and the labour requirements of advanced capitalist production (Sharpe and Green 1975; Bowles and Gintis 1976). By the late 1970s critical theorists argued persuasively that schooling was a central institution to the maintenance and reinforcement of the process of social reproduction.

Alongside these developments in the 1970s was the growing recognition that schooling, as an institution, has also been concerned with the maintenance and reproduction of a sexually differentiated power system. Research focused on the relationship of schooling to the reproduction of the sexual division of labour (Wolpe 1977; Deem 1978; 1980; MacDonald 1981) and the reinforcement of ideologies of femininity and motherhood through overt and covert curricula (Sharpe 1976; Stanworth 1983). Classroom studies contributed to an understanding of how schooling influences the process whereby girls (and boys) emerge from the classroom with gendered identities prepared to take their place in a sexually differentiated society (Spender and Sarah 1980; Spender 1982; Mahony 1985; Weiner 1985). These developments and findings within feminist research reiterated the concerns of the 'new sociology of education': that schooling must be considered within the broad construct of advanced capitalist society. Feminist research argued, however, that schooling must be considered, also in relation to the sexual division of labour (Wolpe 1977; Deem 1980; MacDonald 1980), patriarchal power relations (Spender and Sarah 1980) or the complex integration of the two (Arnot 1982).

It is significant that throughout this work physical education received little attention. It is difficult to identify precisely the reasons for this neglect. One possible, indeed probable explanation is that within many educational circles, physical education has remained of low status academically and consequently has been viewed as having no obvious or significant relationship to the future world of work and the sexual division of labour. Certainly, much of the feminist work on girls' schooling has little direct knowledge of, or involvement with, physical education and few feminist educationalists have a specific background in this area. In addition, research on teachers' attitudes suggests that a large percentage of physical education teachers are unsympathetic towards the notion of equality of opportunity in education (Pratt 1985).

Thus the research project on which the material in this book is based, developed out of a recognition that the area of gender and girls' physical education was under-researched leaving an identifiable gap both in the available literature and in our broader understanding and awareness of the issues surrounding gender and schooling. Furthermore, not only was it important to fill this gap but also I felt convinced that research focusing on gender and physical education could contribute to the broader debates currently developing in feminist theory. Fundamentally, physical education is concerned with many aspects of physical activity and sport. At the onset of the research the area of the 'physical' and the relationship between gender and sport had been largely ignored in feminist work and research. The exceptions to this were the feminist critiques of women's health which included some analysis of the physical, Cynthia Cockburn's (1981) important analysis of physical power relations and the work on women's sport being explored, in particular, by M. Ann Hall (1981; 1984) in Canada and Margaret Talbot (1980) and Jennifer A. Hargreaves (1982) in Britain. However, this latter work tended to be accessible primarily to those involved in sport and physical education rather than to the broader women's movement. Radical feminist work on violence dealt with the reality of male physical power and strength faced by many women (Brownmillar 1975; Dworkin 1981; Wilson 1981). However, the relationships between physicality, the body, violence and sexuality remained under-theorized and there was no attempt to relate critical work on patriarchal relations in sport and physical education to these broader issues of male violence. I felt that this was an exciting and important area ripe for theoretical analysis. Thus, as the seeds of this idea for research on gender and physical education were sown, it was proposed that such a project could contribute to a feminist understanding of a central aspect of girls' schooling *and* to key theoretical debates concerned with male–female power relations.

The identification of the research topic as one of significance in its potential contribution to knowledge in the fields of education and feminist theory did not arise solely out of academic concerns. Three personal factors provided a major impetus for the research investigation. First, I had trained as a physical education teacher in a specialist teacher training college in the late 1960s and subsequently had taught physical education in a city comprehensive school and as head of department in a sixth form college. My considerable experience – as a pupil of physical education in a school, a student at college and as a teacher in secondary schooling – led me to question many aspects of my teaching. While at the sixth form college I became interested in the following questions: Why do many girls opt out of physical activities and sport? Why do girls tend to select 'gender-appropriate' activities? How do my own expectations of 'femininity' influence my teaching? What were my aims for girls' physical education and were they appropriate? Why do some girls, with positive reinforcement and encouragement, become involved and 'successful' in less gender stereotypical activities such as rock climbing, mountaineering or canoeing? What influence did I have as a positive role model? These questions were reaffirmed by a second factor which influenced my choice of research project – a developing feminist consciousness and commitment. My increasing awareness of feminist literature and debates encouraged a critical self-questioning both of my practice as a teacher and my understanding of the importance of the social construction of gender and the implications of expectations of femininity for the structure, content and teaching of girls' physical education. Finally, I was aware that feminist politics appeared in conflict with my personal involvement in physical activity and sport. Many aspects of sporting activity seemed to be viewed negatively by feminists, contributing directly to the construction of a masculinity emphasizing male control, dominance, aggression and competition. There was restricted space for feminist women in this world of male dominance and 'macho' values. Yet I had been involved in sport and physical activities at a variety of competitive and recreational levels since childhood. My own experiences suggested that sport for women *did* possess a liberating potential. Certainly, I felt that it had contributed many positive and enjoyable experiences to my development as a woman, teacher, partner, and so on. Therefore, there was a need to question whether, or how, girls' physical education contributed to and reinforced ideologies of gender (as identified in feminist research into other curriculum areas) and also whether physical education could provide a liberating platform for the challenge to gender relations. It was decided that the focus would be on *girls'* physical education not only because of my personal experiences but also because it remains a distinct and separate curriculum area in most secondary schools. The decision to focus on secondary schooling reflected my own teaching experiences. However, it was felt also that the period of schooling encompassing adolescence is a crucial time for the construction of gender – the period when childhood femininity uneasily approaches the expectations of adult womanhood. This does not deny that primary schooling is a significant influence on the construction and reinforcement of gender-appropriate behaviour but that primary physical education should be the focus of future research.

The aim of the research project, therefore, was to examine how images of 'femininity' and the construction of gender-appropriate behaviour are reinforced and/or challenged by the structure, content and teaching of girls' physical education in secondary schools. The research developed out of personal commitment, experience and interest in the field of study and the identification of an academic area of work which could contribute theoretical knowledge to an under-researched, neglected but important area of understanding and inform future policy initiatives within education.

Structure of the book

Chapter 1 develops the theoretical framework to the research providing an overview of the main feminist theories and their application to the study of gender and schooling. This is an introduction to a vast and continually developing area. Chapter 2 provides the historical context for the research project. Using primary and secondary sources this chapter traces the historical development of girls' physical education from the middle-class girls' schools of the mid-nineteenth century to the current contemporary situation. As this chapter can provide only an historical overview the period from the mid-nineteenth century to early twentieth century receives most attention, for it is here that the roots, foundations and traditions of girls' physical education as a separate subject were laid. The chapter identifies and discusses ideologies of physical ability/capacity, motherhood/domesticity and sexuality which are seen to have become institutionalized in the teaching and content of physical education. Chapters 3 and 4 deal with the contemporary research material. Chapter 3 analyses the responses of the teachers gathered from the interview material. Images and ideas relating to femininity, as identified in the historical section, are considered in order to determine whether similar gender assumptions continue to underpin the teaching of female staff. In order to determine whether images and ideas have become institutionalized in the practice of physical education, Chapter 4 provides details of the school programmes observed in the four case study schools (see Appendix for information on these). These are discussed in relation to organization, staffing, facilities, aims/objectives and curriculum content. Issues relating to gender are identified across all four schools and these form the basis for Chapter 5.

Chapter 5 focuses on three major areas concerning the relationship between gender and girls' physical education. These issues emerge from the historical and contemporary material – co-educational physical education and the implications of organizational change for girls' experiences; ideologies of physicality and the politics of sexuality; young women's sub-cultures, leisure and physical education.

Chapter 6 concludes by considering the theoretical and political implications of the research. The first section focuses on the theoretical debates emerging from the research and discusses its contribution, not only to an increased understanding of gender as a central construct of girls' physical education, but also to how a feminist analysis of girls' physical education can contribute to wider feminist theoretical debates. Finally the chapter looks forward to the implications of the research for future practice. A brief description of the methodology used in the research can be found in the Appendix.

CHAPTER 1

Understanding Gender and Physical Education

It is only since the 1960s, with the resurgence of a strong and committed feminist movement, that issues relating to gender inequalities
have received sustained analytical and political attention. From
consciousness-raising groups through to the political campaigns
around abortion, child-care and violence, women have attempted
to place their experiences at the centre of theoretical analysis and
political action. This has been extended to the development of
intense theoretical debates geared to historical, political and economic analyses of women's positions. Importantly, women have
developed theoretical frameworks around their practice, claiming
that theory can inform practice just as practice must be the cornerstone of theory. This has been the case within education where
feminist researchers and theorists have investigated and explained
gender inequalities within various aspects of the schooling process.

As discussed in the introduction, however, physical education
remains conspicuous by its absence in most of these analyses. Yet it
is important to explore the full potential of feminist theory in developing an understanding of gender and physical education. First it is
necessary to clarify the distinction between the terms *sex* and *gender.* Ann Oakley (1972) offers a commonly accepted definition
referring to 'sex' as the biological 'condition' of being female or
male and to 'gender' as the social/cultural/psychological processes
through which femininity and masculinity are constructed and
reproduced. Using this definition it is acknowledged that 'gender' is
not constant and varies across cultures, throughout history and during the life cycle of an individual. The distinction between 'sex' and
'gender' is important because many divisions and differences

between women and men, girls and boys are popularly considered
to be the result of *sex* differences.

There is a commonly held, fundamental assertion of the 'natural-
ness' of such divisions stemming from biological difference. Thus
differences in girls' and boys' physical education, their participation
and their performance often are explained in terms of natural,
biological physical differences. But there is now considerable
material, dealing specifically with the extension of women's opportunities in sport, which has challenged popular assumptions and
academic 'truths' concerning physiological or 'natural' sex differences. Two of the main researchers at the forefront of this challenge
have been Elizabeth Ferris (1978) and Ken Dyer (1982). They drew
on a number of research projects throughout the world which measured such physiological features as maximum oxygen uptake,
stamina, strength and hormonal differences. This together with
their own empirical research, raised serious doubts, if not refuted,
the commonly held and taken-for-granted assumptions concerning
physical/physiological sex differences. However, while this work
has been important in challenging myths surrounding physical sex
differences, it provides only a stepping-stone to more central work
on gender *relations*. Paul Willis argued against the developing
emphasis on a sex *difference* approach as early as 1974:

> The analytical socio-cultural task is not to measure these differences
> precisely and explain them physically, but to ask why some differ-
> ences, and not others, are taken as so important, become so exagger-
> ated, are used to buttress social attitudes or prejudice. (Willis
> 1974: 3)

The acknowledgement that it is the *social construction of gender*
that is important, not biological differences, allows the development of a more critical and adequate understanding of gender
inequalities in sport and physical education, locating the debate
within the wider power structures of society.

This research, therefore, took the social construction of gender as
its starting-point asserting the centrality of inequalities of
opportunities, access and outcomes which potentially restrict and
oppress girls and young women during their experiences of physical
education in schools. There are certain characteristics associated
with stereotypical views of femininity and masculinity which
strongly reinforce the expectations of what is appropriate for girls

and women, boys and men, at different ages. In state institutions, such as schools, these images are consolidated and reproduced as ideologies which form the basis for the political management of gender divisions in wider society.

However, it should not be assumed that the existence of gender stereotypes is all-determining, resulting in the conformity of all girls and boys to expected roles, behaviour and attitudes. Clearly, many individuals challenge the process of gender stereotyping – not always consciously – and as a consequence the transmission of stereotypes is by no means simplistic, absolute or uncontested. Yet the strength and pervasiveness of common-sense assumptions about what it means 'to be a girl' or 'to be a boy' cannot be underestimated. While the definitions of femininity and masculinity may vary, the extent of gender-specific assumptions, which collectively lend support to powerful dominant ideologies, have considerable impact on cultural and institutional practice. In the development of a coherent analysis of gender and physical education, it is important to examine the means by which dominant ideologies of femininity and masculinity have consequences for, and are reinforced by, the priorities, policies and practices of physical education in the institution of schooling. This suggests that the relationship between gender and physical education, and the social and political construction of 'physicality', with all that implies for relations of dominance and dependency, should be central rather than peripheral to broader feminist theory and politics.

Feminist theory and physical education

In her discussion of feminism, Helen Roberts (1981: 15) comments that in the first place it is an attempt to insist upon the very experience and very existence of women. Within this framework a 'feminist position' can be identified which is shared by different theoretical perspectives. Dorothy Smith (1977) suggests that there are three central premises in the development of a feminist analysis:

> One is that a feminist takes the standpoint of women . . . we begin with ourselves with our sense of what we are, our own experience. The second is that we oppose women's oppression . . . And the third thing is the recognition of sisterhood. (Smith 1977: 2)

'Sisterhood' suggests a shared experience of oppression which is based on being a woman. This shared experience, however, is felt at different levels of intensity depending on particular situations. While acknowledging the fundamental aspects of a feminist position it is at this point that feminists diverge. Critical questions relating to the primary source of women's oppression result in several strands of feminist theory each of which gives primacy to different factors. Sandra Acker et al. (1984) make a useful distinction between 'implementary' approaches and 'fundamental' approaches. They suggest that 'implementary' approaches

> do not address questions about the underlying reasons for the domi-
> nation/subordination patterns; instead, they ask about how individ-
> uals in a given culture go about learning and perpetuating such
> arrangements. (Acker et al. 1984: 66)

These approaches tend to be categorized as 'liberal' or 'equal opportunities' feminism and are concerned with issues around socialization and challenging discriminatory practices. 'Fundamental approaches' differ in that they

> seek basic, universal explanations: they ask what features of human
> nature or social organization require or demand that women be sub-
> ordinate. (Acker et al. 1984: 68)

At the heart of these approaches is the recognition of a power structure whereby women are placed in a subordinate position. These approaches can be further subdivided into those which identify class divisions and the economic structure of advanced capitalism as the primary source of women's oppression (Marxist feminism); those which place patriarchal power relations centrally (radical feminism and also separatist feminism); those which combine class–sex issues in an attempt to integrate or accommodate the structural relations of advanced capitalism within their analysis (socialist feminism). It is important to stress that this framework, although well used, is a schematic and simplistic categorization of what have become complex and heavily debated theoretical standpoints. The debates have been marked not only between, but also within, these broad positions. Furthermore, black feminists have stressed that the British, European and 'Commonwealth' legacies are those derived from imperialism, nationalism and the history of colonization. Current critical analysis of gender, therefore, cannot ignore these legacies and their current manifestation especially the consolidation of institutionalized racism within the structural relations of 'neo-colonialism'.

The different standpoints of liberal, radical, Marxist, socialist feminism reflect different emphases but fundamentally they each accept that women are oppressed and are subordinate to men in many aspects of their lives and that this process is reinforced by political, economic and social institutions. Non-feminist approaches to physical education would not prioritize gender relations in their analyses nor would they seek to understand how physical education contributes to the structural and ideological shaping of women's oppression. However, it was the starting-point of this research that in order to overcome or indeed challenge women's oppression, institutional settings such as schools, must be investigated and gender inequalities identified. The main theoretical focus, therefore, centred on a feminist approach with an initial consideration of how each feminist theoretical perspective could contribute to an understanding of gender relations and physical education.

Liberal feminism

The primary characteristic of liberal feminism is its emphasis on sex discrimination, 'equal opportunities' and 'women's rights'. The broad social context is not seen as a power structure which prevents women from gaining equality with men. The focus is far more on the presence of the social practices of discrimination and socialization which create prejudice and, ultimately, inequality. Within this framework there is considerable optimism, for if discriminatory laws are challenged and changed, socialization practices altered and consciousness at an individual level raised, then women will gain the equal status to which they aspire. What the perspective assumes is that the social arrangements within 'democratic societies' are fundamentally sound but that certain adjustments – such as gender equality – need to be made, thus removing aberrant and outdated discriminatory practices. In liberal feminist approaches to physical education, attention is centred on the differentiation of activities – the socialization of girls into 'female' activities, for example gymnastics and netball, and boys into 'male' activities, for example football and cricket (Inner London Education Authority 1984).

Discriminatory practices relating to clothing for physical education lessons, the stereotyping of girls and boys by physical education teachers, unequal access to facilities and extra-curricular time
and differential career structures of female and male physical education teachers have each received attention (see, for example,
Inner London Education Authority 1984; Leaman 1984; Evans and
Williams 1988).

From a liberal feminist perspective, future non-sexist practice is
derived in increased opportunities and a concerted challenge to discrimination and the raising of consciousness as an effective challenge to stereotyping. This is a relatively optimistic approach to
gender relations because reform is the goal within a social system
based on the principles of liberal democracy which interpret 'power'
as pluralized among healthy, competing interests.

This approach to gender and physical education tends to see the
'problem' to be in the attitudes and practices of the female pupils and
women physical education teachers. However, as critics of this position argue, reforms at the 'micro' level of individual teachers, pupils
or even local education authorities through consciousness-raising
and anti-discriminatory practices, may provide immediate benefit
for those involved but will fail to produce long-term solutions, for
they neglect the significance of broader structural relations. As
Gaby Weiner explains:

> The principal aim of this equal opportunities approach was to
> encourage girls to move into privileged and senior positions in
> *existing* educational institutions rather than seek any fundamental
> changes in schooling . . . to liberalize access to an inadequate system
> might be acceptable in the short term but for more permanent change
> a major restructuring of all social institutions including schools is
> needed. (Weiner 1985: 8, 10, emphasis added)

These concerns directed towards fundamental change and restructuring in physical education are central to more 'radical' theories and
standpoints.

Radical feminism

Radical feminists are unified in their concentration on the power
relationships between men and women as fundamental to the
oppression of women. They use the concept of 'patriarchy' to

develop a systematic explanation of the structural relations of oppession whereby men dominate women in a complex arena of power relations. It is this notion of *patriarchal* power relations which places radical feminist theory in a critical framework absent in liberal feminism. 'Patriarchy', therefore, is central to radical feminism and is defined most usually as an all-pervasive system of male power domination (Millet 1971). By focusing on male domination, radical feminists have raised questions concerned with education in relation to what constitutes acceptable knowledge (Spender 1982); the dominance of boys in classroom practice whereby they monopolize teacher attention, linguistic space and physical space (Clarricoates 1982; Spender 1982; Mahony 1985); and the use of girls' appearance and sexuality for disciplinary purposes (Llewellyn 1980; Griffin 1985).

Probably the most influential work from a radical feminist perspective applicable to physical education is that which focuses on sexuality as being fundamental to the subordination and oppression of women (Lenskyj 1986). Catherine MacKinnon makes the point:

> Sexuality is a form of power. Gender as socially constructed embodies it, not the reverse. Women and men are divided by gender, made into the sexes as we know them, by the sexual requirements of heterosexuality, which institutionalizes male sexual dominance and female sexual submission. If this is true, sexuality is the lynchpin of gender inequality. (MacKinnon 1982: 533)

Radical feminists, therefore, argue that male sexuality functions to control women in work, sport, leisure, social space, schooling, and so on. This control operates both in the private and public spheres and benefits all men regardless of their desires and objectives. Thus a radical analysis of physical education emphasizes the means and processes by which physical education reinforces and reproduces female and male heterosexuality. Through physical education girls and young women learn a female 'physicality' which emphasizes appearance, presentation and control (desirable 'femininity'), while boys are encouraged to develop physical strength, aggression and confidence in their physical prowess (desirable 'masculinity'). It is these connections between physical activity, sexuality, physicality and gender power relations (women's oppression) which are central to this theoretical approach.

A challenge to gender inequality from this radical position would involve far more than institutional reform. For many radical feminist educationalists the initial step towards this challenge must involve 'girl-centred organization'. Pat Mahony maintains that it is the relationship between men and women that has to be changed if women are to move out of an oppressed situation. The implication for girls schooling is unambiguous:

> co-education, as things stand, is not more socially desirable for girls because it is more normal. Rather it is because it is more normal it is, for girls, highly undesirable. (Mahony 1985: 93)

The separatist arguments which have formed a central position within radical feminist analysis are particularly interesting for physical education. Traditionally at secondary school level in Britain, girls' physical education has been maintained as a separate sphere controlled by women for female pupils. However, the moves towards co-educational physical education and the changes in teacher training over the past few decades (Fletcher 1984) have brought into stark relief the issue of single-sex provision from a radical feminist theoretical standpoint. This will be developed further in Chapter 5.

Marxist feminism

Marxist feminist theoretical explanations are part of the broader Marxist framework which situates gender relations within the context of the social reproduction of class relations. Women are seen to be oppressed because of their role within the family and the sexual division of labour. Marxist feminists identify the relationship of the family to the capitalist mode of production as central to their theses. The oppression of women is a product of the class system and the private ownership of property. Thus the primary battle must be that waged against an oppressive economic class system. Change in the lives and experiences of women will result only from a radical change in the economic structure of society. Women must work alongside the working class as a whole, if fundamental change is to be achieved. While there is minimal feminist work in the area, the main stress of Marxist writers and researchers in physical education is on the part it plays in the reproduction of capitalist values (Hargreaves 1986). Physical education is seen to have developed from the values of the late-nineteenth-century bourgeoisie, with the emphasis for boys on the 'character-building' elements of physical activity and the centrality of 'competition'. Physical education, therefore, contributes to the reproduction of the values and attitudes needed for the future workers in capitalist societies. Physical education for girls is seen to be premised on the relationship between physical health and motherhood. Again, historical analysis is fundamental to Marxist feminist explanations. Girls' physical education is identified as developing out of a desire to ensure that the mothers of the future generation were physically fit to produce healthy workers. Contemporary physical education is placed within this historical context, recognizing that through the reinforcement of femininity and masculinity, it functions as a main determining agent in the reproduction of a sexual division of labour.

Critics of Marxist feminist standpoints argue that the analysis is over-deterministic, failing to pay sufficient attention to the importance of resistance and agency. The reproduction of class and gender relations is by no means simplistic, straightforward or predetermined. People can and do challenge the social system and critics argue that this resistance is largely ignored or under-theorized.

The major criticism of Marxist feminist analysis, including that pertaining to physical education, is that it tends to ignore or under-theorize the concept of patriarchal domination and control. It fails to explain why gender divisions benefit capital, why divisions have to be sexual divisions or why women need to be subordinate to men. Many Marxist feminists have begun to question whether gender *can* be located simplistically in a class analysis. There is a developing concern to understand the ways in which schooling (including physical education) is involved in the reproduction of *both* class and gender relations under capitalism. This has led to the next theoretical position to be considered: socialist feminism.

Socialist feminism

Socialist feminists attempt to combine elements of a Marxist feminist approach with a radical feminist approach, thus arguing for an understanding of both patriarchal oppression and class oppression. The relationship between patriarchy and capitalism is the crucial issue. Some theorists argue that the most useful theoretical framework is a unified system which comprehends capitalist patriarchy as one system, with the oppression of women an essential and fundamental characteristic of that system (Eisenstein 1979; Young 1981). Others favour a 'dual systems' theory which acknowledges the existence of two systems which exist separately but are in continual interaction (Hartmann 1979; Cockburn 1983). In whatever way the relationship between sex and class is theoretically argued, the understanding of gender relations within capitalist society is drawn from neo-Marxist approaches rather than the economic determinism of classical Marxism. These analyses stress the importance of the role of ideology and social reproduction rather than economic reductionism. More emphasis is placed on the 'superstructure' (i.e. social, cultural, political and ideological levels) in providing the conditions for capitalist production to proceed.

The relationship between gender and class remains the subject of a complex ongoing debate. Socialist feminists, therefore, draw on the work of both Marxist and radical feminist theorists with gender either situated alongside class (recognizing a *dual* system of oppression, i.e. patriarchy *and* capitalism), or as a unified, integrated system which recognizes the universality of patriarchal relations within social systems (capitalist patriarchy). In physical education socialist feminist theory highlights the importance of historical analysis in identifying the roots of contemporary teaching. Ideologies of masculinity and femininity, particularly those relating to physicality, motherhood and sexuality, are central to an understanding of the relationship between gender and physical education. However, the experiences of girls in physical education are seen also to be dependent on their class location. The subject needs to be situated within the context of the reproduction of a sexual division of leisure, fundamental to any analysis of advanced capitalism in the late twentieth century. This sexual division of leisure is experienced differently for working-class and middle-class girls and young women. For example, differential access to transport, facilities, sports clubs and so on influences out-of-school opportunities and experiences of physical activity.

The main critics of this position argue that the theoretical analysis of the relationship between gender and class remains underdeveloped. However, by recognizing the importance of *both* gender *and* class relations, whether as a dual structure or an integrated system, socialist feminists argue that a more comprehensive insight into the conditions necessary for change can be achieved. A challenge to both capitalist and patriarchal relations requires both short-term strategies for reform alongside more long-term plans for radi-cal structural change. The argument is that unless ideologies of femininity and masculinity (incorporating physical power relations, sexuality *and* the sexual division of labour) are challenged and altered in and through physical education, then gender divisions and inequalities will continue to be produced and reproduced.

Finally, a criticism that has been levelled at all feminist theoretical positions concerns the issue that 'race' continues to be ignored or marginalized.

Gender and 'race'

Black feminists (Carby 1982; Hooks 1982; 1989; Amos and Parmar 1984) have identified the ethnocentrism of much feminist analysis and research. Research into gender and schooling is no exception. There is little work in physical education theory that considers 'race', and the limited amount of research that does investigate gen-der, 'race' and physical education has tended to concentrate on a cultural approach (Carrington et al. 1987; Carrington and Williams 1988). This work is problematical, in that it focuses on how gender differences in school physical education and community leisure activities may be heightened by ethnicity. There is an identification of stereotypical perceptions held by many teachers that South Asian boys are very good at cricket and enthusiastic about weight training and self-defence. This confirms other racial stereotyping which assumes that Afro-Caribbean children naturally excel at certain sporting and athletic events. Furthermore, the research by Carring-ton and Williams (1988) emphasizes the cultural pressures on Asian girls, exerted by parents, which restrict their participation in co-educational activities (especially swimming), their involvement in extra-curricular pursuits and the problems associated with 'suit-able' dress for physical education.

However, what is missing from research concerning gender, 'race' and physical education is a thorough analysis of the politics of 'race' and racism, and the complex interrelationship of gender and 'race' within the contextual framework of structures of patriarchy and neo-colonialism. It is this neglect that has been identified and criti-cized by black feminists. In physical education (as in other research into 'race'), there is a danger that research and analysis identifies a 'problem' which is seen to relate to cultural *difference*. Yet in relation

to physical education the issue for pupils and teachers from culturally distinct backgrounds centres, not only on stereotyping and
teacher–pupil expectations, but also on the reinforcement and
reproduction of institutional racism through physical education
teaching. The 'problem' is the ethnocentrism of schooling and individuals and institutional racism rather than the cultural diversity of
pupils.

In Britain, girls and young women who experience racism (Afro-
Caribbean, South Asian, Irish, Chinese, etc.) experience gender
inequalities and oppression mediated by 'race' and racism. Many
aspects of gender cut across racial divisions, but the extent to which
racial inequalities and oppression interact with gender in some
instances remains under-researched and under-theorized.

In conclusion to this introduction to feminist theoretical analysis,
I would add that there is a recognition that feminist theory cannot be
categorized neatly into the sections labelled liberal, radical, Marxist
and socialist. Relationships, interconnections and the need to
explain the experiences of *all* women suggest a complex overlapping
of positions in many instances. Theory is fluid and changing and
theory develops from previous ideas and knowledge. Thus the
categorization used is convenient for explanation but should not be
considered rigid and inflexible. Furthermore, feminist theory has
developed from these early debates and now the voices of psy-
choanalytical feminism (Kristeva 1982) and poststructural feminist
theories (Weedon 1987); among others, are of increasing significance. However, the work of feminists throughout the 1970s and
1980s which I have introduced in this chapter provided the influential theoretical frameworks from which my research developed. My
research project on gender and physical education started from a
theoretical position which acknowledged both patriarchy and capitalism as dual systems of oppression. The importance of power
relations, both between women and men and between women of
different class locations, is acknowledged although the points of
interconnection, conflict and contradiction remain problematic.
Schools as important institutions serve to reproduce the status quo
in relation to the capitalist mode of production and male–female
power relations, albeit within a complex and often contested situation. Physical education as an aspect of schooling fits into this process both in terms of its relationship to a sexual division of leisure in
society and the reinforcement of patriarchal power relations. These

power relations need to be considered in terms of their economic, social, political, ideological and physical aspects. The empirical case work material was approached from this dual position and the implications that this material has for developing a fuller theoretical framework form the conclusion to the research. The emphases and complexities identified by detailed empirical investigation provide the cornerstone for the development of greater understanding of the position of women in physical education and, ultimately, the relationship of this to the overall position of women within a society which is both patriarchal and capitalist. All feminist analysis begins from the premise that gender involves inequality and oppression, an understanding of which provides the basis for political action and change.

CHAPTER 2

The Historical Context

As with much historical literature, physical education accounts have tended to concentrate on the experiences of boys. Many girls' and women's experiences remain 'hidden from history' (Rowbotham 1973). A comprehensive history of physical education, which incorporates the central role of gender and places the development of physical education within a social, economic and political context, is yet to be fully developed. It is beyond the scope of this chapter to provide such a comprehensive analysis. However, it is important to reflect on the years of innovation when physical education first entered the formal institutions of schooling. For it was here that the traditions and ideologies, fundamental to the ethos and emphases of physical education, found root and grew as the subject became consolidated and integrated within the schooling system.

Any historical account is fraught with difficulty. The relationships within official discourses, found in laws, documents, texts and practical outcomes, cannot be taken at face value. An overly deterministic analysis does not allow for individual responses and negotiations between schools, teachers and pupils. The outcome of stated policies do not necessarily match the prescribed intentions. As Rosemary Deem (1981) comments:

> It should also be remembered in connection with ideologies about women, that just as policies still have to be interpreted by local authorities, and individual schools, so ideologies still have to be translated into specific policies and practices and this may lead to inconsistencies. Hence, for example, in the case of the educational system, we should not assume that dominant ideologies about

women necessarily give rise to uniform practices in schools and among teachers. (Deem 1981: 132)

It is important, however, to identify ideologies about women and consider whether such ideologies have consequences for social practice. While acknowledging that there is no easy relationship between intentions and outcomes, it is reasonable to assume that ideas and images, which are inherent in the structure and development of a subject, have the potential to exert real influence on those who experience its policies and practice, while retaining an awareness of the possibility of contestation.

The foundations of girls' physical education

To the importance of bodily exercise most people are in the same degree awake. Perhaps less needs saying on this requisite of physical education than on most others; at any rate in so far as boys are concerned. (Spencer 1861: 151–2)

Herbert Spencer, writing in the mid-nineteenth century, noted an 'astonishing difference' between the 'natural spontaneous activity' prevalent in boys' education and the limited system of 'factitious exercise – gymnastics' which appeared the sole provision in female educational establishments. He argued that the justification for physical education was for health and happiness and considered that

For girls as well as boys, the sportive activities to which the instincts impel are essential to bodily welfare. Whoever forbids them, forbids the divinely-appointed means to physical development. (Spencer 1861: 155)

He considered the link between mind and body as essential to the development of physical education and argued that the effects of intellectual study and over-concentration of the mind, without similar commitment to the health of the body, was extremely damaging.

Being in great measure debarred from those vigorous and enjoyable exercises of body by which boys mitigate the evils of excessive study, girls feel these evils in their full intensity. Hence, the much smaller proportion of them who grow up well made and healthy. In the pale, angular, flat-chested young ladies, so abundant in London drawing

rooms, we see the effect of merciless application, unrelieved by
youthful sports; and this physical degeneracy hinders their welfare
far more than their many accomplishments. (Spencer 1861: 186–7)

Physical degeneracy and the importance of nature were fundamental considerations in Spencer's writing. While a major proclaimant
of Social Darwinism and the theory of conservation of energy,
his emphasis on a healthy body and a sound mind was in no way
incompatible with his desire to see an improved system of physical
education for girls.

At the time Spencer was making his observations only minimal
physical exercise was provided in the limited schooling available to
older girls. The private schools and establishments included little
more than callisthenics or gentle exercises. This was well illustrated
by the Schools Inquiry Commission (1868), which examined one
hundred private schools for girls and disclosed that while thirty-two
provided nothing but callisthenics, sixty-six offered only 'walking
abroad, croquet and dancing'. During the 1850s the first two day
high schools for girls were founded at North London Collegiate
(1850) and Cheltenham Ladies College (1853). It was in the climate
of such restricted opportunities for girls that physical education was
developed. The growth of physical education was paralleled and
influenced by changes in the position of women in society and the
increased involvement of women in physical exercises and sporting
activity in general. However, change did not occur swiftly or without fierce opposition. Battles over physical activity for women were
fought both in and outside educational settings and, as the following section will discuss, were implicitly linked to ideas and
common-sense assumptions about women's 'natural' and desirable
characteristics.

Moreover, the fact that changes did occur was partly due to the
development of a newly devised system of Swedish exercises and the
work of Martina Bergman-Osterberg. In 1879 Concordia Lofving
was invited by her employers, the London School Board, to introduce the Ling system into London schools. These exercises developed in Sweden by the gymnast Per Ling were based on far more
scientific principles of movement than previously had been considered. After one year, Martina Bergman (later Bergman-Osterberg)
replaced Concordia Lofving in the post and began to train teachers
in the Swedish system. When she left this post in 1887 she had trained

1,312 teachers in this method and all the Board schools were familiar with the Ling system. However, it was Bergman-Osterberg's opening of a training college for teachers of physical education, in Hampstead in 1885 (the college moved to Dartford in 1895), which exerted the greatest influence on the teaching of physical education in secondary schools. This was the forerunner of the women's specialist teacher training colleges established in the following decade: 1897 Anstey; 1903 Bedford; 1895 Chelsea; 1900 I.M. Marsh. The initial aim of Dartford College was to introduce Ling's scientific movement into the school curriculum and replace the callisthenics and musical drill which remained the main exercise for girls in most schools. In 1899 Bergman-Osterberg extolled the virtues of a female physical education teacher:

> Let us once and for all discard man as a physical trainer of women . . .
> let us send the drill sargeant right-about-face to his awkward squad.
> This work we women do better, as our very success in training
> depends upon our having felt like women, able to calculate the
> possibilities of our sex, knowing our weakness and our strength.
> (cited in Fletcher 1984: 31)

Thus the female physical educationalist emerged and had a major influence on the development of girls' physical education over the next century, as a separate, independent female subject in the curricula of secondary schools. The two-year course at Dartford College included gynmastics, outdoor games, swimming, fencing, anatomy, physiology, hygiene, medical gymnastics, theory of movement, anthropometry and practical teaching of physical education (Hargreaves 1979: 156). A comprehensive and balanced system of physical education had been devised and its influence filtered into the secondary schools.

From the outset the introduction of team games into the curriculum was controversial. The first girls' high schools at North London Collegiate and Cheltenham Ladies College (headed by the Misses Buss and Beale respectively) had quickly adopted Swedish exercises into their curriculum but were more reticent about the value of team games. The eventual acceptance of team games was influenced by developments in women's recreation and the organization of outdoor sports throughout Britain during the latter part of the nineteenth century. Miss Buss was more enthusiastic about team games than her colleague at Cheltenham, reflecting the different school philosophies. She introduced a games club during the dinner break and by the 1890s she included several outdoor games – hockey, netball and tennis – in the widening physical education curriculum. Miss Beale was less committed to team games and initially opposed their inclusion in the curriculum. However, mounting pressure eventually forced Miss Beale to concede and in 1896 she ordered the acquisition of land in order to develop playing fields (Purvis 1991: 87–8). By the late 1890s the students were playing rounders, cricket and hockey.

The new girls' public schools were more enthusiastic about outdoor games adopting many features of the male curriculum and its objectives, including their emphasis on team games with their *esprit de corps*, morality and character-building potential (see Mangan 1982). Penelope Lawrence (1898: 145), headmistress of Roedean, saw the 'close connection between a strong, vigorous, well-balanced body with a strong, vigorous and well-balanced mind'. She considered games to be 'more satisfactory than any other exercise', being important in 'training character'. By the turn of the century cricket, hockey, tennis, fives and rounders were played at Roedean. While Roedean placed most emphasis on games and physical activity, similar developments were taking place at other boarding schools (e.g. St Leonards, Wycombe Abbey and St Andrews).

By the early years of the twentieth century a comprehensive system of physical education involving organized games and Swedish gymnastics was accepted by the girls' secondary schools. It was the middle-class establishments which were the prime recipients of these innovations. However, older girls in the elementary system did benefit from the initial work of Bergman-Osterberg in the London Board of Schools and eventually the Ling system of exercises was established throughout most of the elementary schools in England and Wales. Facilities for outdoor games, plus expertise in teaching, were lacking in most of the schools for working-class girls and it was a considerable time before they benefited from the more thorough system of physical education available to their middle-class 'sisters'.

The development of girls' physical education was associated with various factors: changing economic systems; increased opportunities in women's sporting activities; the innovations of the Swedish system of exercise and, later, the development of specialist teacher training establishments. The ethos around games-playing transferred from the male public boarding schools to the new girls' public schools with a general commitment to, and concern for, health and physical welfare of the body. This final association was fundamental to the introduction of physical education in secondary schools and continued throughout its future development. Just as Herbert Spencer (1861) had emphasized the importance of health and the relationship between a healthy mind and a healthy body, so the early physical educationalists related their work to scientific principles of medicine. From the beginning they incorporated remedial and therapeutic work into their programmes of physical exercise. Teachers of physical education who left the newly formed teacher training colleges were qualified to teach in schools and to undertake work in remedial gymnastics, massage and therapeutic activities in private clinics or hospitals. In schools this association with medicine encouraged regular physical examinations and medical inspections both by school doctors and physical education staff. As Jennifer Hargreaves (1979) argues:

> good health was the conditional starting point for the education of girls, and the physical education mistress became established as the schools' supreme caretaker of the girls' bodies. (Hargreaves 1979: 175)

The influence of the predominantly male medical profession continued into the twentieth century. The formal links between medical practitioners and physical education in the girls' high schools were somewhat tenuous. However, as physical education slowly filtered into the state system, the influence of the medical department of the Board of Education, set up in 1908 under Sir George Newman, became far more important. From this time the supervision of physical training was in the hands of the medical department, which became responsible for policy recommendations and the establishment of syllabuses used to direct the teaching in the schools.

By 1914, and the outbreak of the First World War, physical education was established formally within the secondary school system for girls. It was a relatively comprehensive system including gymnastics, swimming, outdoor games and some dancing. In the elementary system, older girls were less fortunate, although many received instruction in the Swedish system with emphasis on the therapeutic nature of such exercise. These were the foundations from which the comprehensive system of physical education emerged in the post-1944 'secondary education of all' era. Before considering the changes in physical education during this gradual increase in provision of secondary schooling, it is necessary to assess these foundations more critically.

As with the emergence of opportunities for girls' secondary schooling in general, it is important to consider the ideological framework which incorporated these developments. Physical education did not enter the schooling system in a vacuum. Its entrance was affected by, and dependent upon, gender and class ideologies which influenced the material outcomes of its development. Class differentiation resulted in a system of privileged schooling under which the daughters of the middle and the upper classes were the first to obtain the opportunities to exercise and develop their bodies in a way previously considered impossible. Yet gender-based ideologies cut across class boundaries. Whereas working-class girls were restricted through their class location, all girls experienced a system of physical activity developed according to ideas and images held about desirable and acceptable gender-specific behaviour, roles and characteristics. These gender images were defined differently according to specific class locations but it is the gender ideologies of middle-class femininity, motherhood and sexuality which underpinned the foundation and development of a comprehensive system of girls' physical education.

Femininity

> This priority of bodily training is common to both sexes but it is directed to a different object. In the case of boys the object is to develop strength, in the case of girls to bring about their charms . . . Women need enough strength to act gracefully, men enough skill to act easily. (Rousseau, quoted in Archer 1964: 221)

During the nineteenth century, the dominant image of the Victorian 'lady' was that of a weak helpless creature who 'was incapable and ultimately disabled such that she must be protected and prohibited from serious participation in society' (Duffin 1978: 26). It was the myth of 'woman as invalid' (Ehrenrich and English 1975) which was challenged by early feminists in order to establish access to schooling, higher education and, ultimately, the social and economic liberation of women. Women's 'physical' liberation was an important aspect of the feminist cause, for some of the key characteristics of 'femininity' which needed to be challenged, related to women's supposed 'natural' physical inferiority, weakness and passivity. The demand for educational opportunities for women challenged the perceived incompatability between femininity and learning. Indeed it was important to demonstrate that women could be sufficiently fit to undertake sustained mental work. The philosophy of a 'fit mind in a fit body' was fundamental to the beginnings of middle-class girls' secondary schooling. Yet it remains in doubt just how far the development of physical education challenged Rousseau's view that bodily training for girls needed to be quite different from that for boys. This philosophy was based on biological explanations of sex differences, with the emphasis for girls on developing 'charm' and 'grace' – attributes essential for a 'feminine' woman. The 'establishments' for young ladies in the early years of the nineteenth century certainly had used physical exercise to this end. Ladylike accomplishments, so much the purpose of this limited schooling, emphasized physical exercise for young women to develop the grace and beauty befitting a young lady. Frances Cobbe (1894), an early pioneer for women's right to schooling, recalled:

> Beside the dancing we had 'callisthenic' lessons every week from a 'Capitaine'. Somebody, who puts us through manifold exercises with poles and dumb-bells. How much better a few country scrambles would have been than all those callisthenics it is needless to say, but our dismal walks were confined to parading the esplanade and neighbouring terraces. (quoted in Murray 1982: 201–2)

This was the accepted physical exercise for all middle and upper-class women, as reflected in Donald Walker's (1834) treatise *Exercises for Ladies*. This encouraged 'ladies' to use their recreation to develop 'ladylike' qualities of beauty and deportment, using wands and dumbbells in gentle swinging motions.

As discussed earlier, during the late nineteenth century Swedish gymnastics became an integral part of physical education programmes for girls in secondary schooling. While this represented a shift towards a more energetic system of movements than previously promoted by callisthenics, it retained a commitment to the ideology of women's 'natural' biologically determined abilities. Ling, who introduced and developed the Swedish system, emphasized the importance of maintaining the 'natural' abilities of women without inducing undue strain or unwelcome physical changes. Central to his system was the assumption that women's

> physiological predisposition demands less vigorous treatment. The *law of beauty* is based purely on the conception of line and must not be abused. *The rounded forms of women must not be transformed into angularity or nodosity such as in man.* (quoted in Webb 1967: 49, emphases added)

The pre-set, presumably biological, 'law of beauty', together with women's 'natural' predisposition to 'rounded forms' were taken-for-granted assumptions which lay at the heart of the ideology of biology underpinning the institutionalization of physical education for girls.

Towards the end of the nineteenth century, the introduction of team games into girls' public schooling, initiated by the developing public schools (Roedean, Wycombe Abbey, St Leonards) offered a much stronger challenge to assumptions and images of femininity. Indeed the vigorous physical activity needed for team games was the antithesis of femininity. Yet while imitating the boys' public schools, the inclusion of team games was premised on the assumption that girls needed to be given different experiences. At no time was it considered appropriate to provide the same physical activities as those enjoyed by their public school brothers. The games of the girls' public schools remained within the bounds of acceptable 'feminine' behaviour. This does not deny that changes in the definition of 'femininity' were taking place. By the late nineteenth century the new 'high schools' and the girls' public schools represented a real challenge to the Victorian ideal of the 'feminine' woman. Yet Penelope Lawrence (1898), headmistress of Roedean, stressed that they must 'rigorously exclude games with vulgar and vicious associations' and while the 'new' woman engaged in games, they were adapted or foreshortened. Ultimately there was an acceptance of innate physical differences between men and women, thus limiting girls' access to those sports which stressed endurance, strength or physical contact. Consequently, 'male' sports were adapted to accommodate women's 'innate' abilities and new sports were introduced such as netball, lacrosse and hockey, which 'did not carry the stigma of overt masculinity' (McCrone 1982: 28).

The incorporation of team games into the school curriculum received opposition from both within and outside the school system. Dorothea Beale, headmistress of Cheltenham Ladies College, encouraged the development of girls' opportunities in schooling yet vehemently opposed outdoor games and competition in general. She 'grudgingly allowed for the introduction of team games but would not allow inter-school competition' (Atkinson 1978). Her position was clear:

> I am most anxious the girls should not over-exert themselves or become absorbed in athletic rivalries, and therefore we do not play against other schools. (quoted in Kamm 1958: 223)

Her dislike for games and competition reflected the view that they were incompatible with womanliness. Gentility and dignity were high priorities throughout all aspects of girls' schooling at Cheltenham and it was feared that they would be challenged by competitive physical exercise. Games were equated with masculinity and seen to be antithetical to desirable female characteristics. However, not all schools were opposed to team games *per se*. At St Leonards games were considered to encourage beauty, grace and good health; indeed it was asserted that girls could play very rough games without becoming unwomanly. Thus, the issue was not the desirability of reinforcing or encouraging 'femininity' or 'womanly qualities', rather the arguments focused on whether games playing could occur without a serious challenge to young women's femininity. Many schools encouraged team games but in a form deemed 'appropriate' for girls and young women which incorporated an ideology of femininity.

As the twentieth century arrived team games had become accepted into many high schools and most girls' public schools. Their acceptance was counterbalanced by an emphasis on 'ladylike' qualities when off the playing field. The histories of the training of women physical education teachers illustrate this point most effectively (see, for example, Crunden 1974; Fletcher 1984). As Miss Dove, headmistress of both St Leonards School and Wycombe Abbey School, stated to a colleague: 'Your ladies play like gentlemen, and behave like ladies' (quoted in Hargreaves 1979: 138). Therefore, the system of physical education incorporating games and gymnastics, accommodated common-sense assumptions about femininity by offering different opportunities to girls for physical exercise. These opportunities involved negotiation and compromise but, ultimately adapting to, rather than fundamentally challenging the biologically determined arguments relating to women's physical ability and capacity. The ethos of 'differential' physical education for girls was firmly established during the early years of its development.

Motherhood

The ideology of motherhood, with its central image of women as 'guardian of the race', was an integral part of the ethos of girls' secondary schooling. The concern was to encourage healthy growth in mind and body in order to ensure the health and well-being of future generations. Consequently the relationship between teaching and motherhood was stressed throughout physical education teacher training.

> If every mother and every teacher had a rational understanding of the value of physical exercise, based on anatomical and physiological laws; if to this was added a practical knowledge of personal hygiene, a long step would be taken to solve some of our present difficulties and problems. (Bergman-Osterberg, cited in Fletcher 1984: 35)

Guaranteeing the health of the nation was tied into the role and function of motherhood. Girls received physical education to ensure healthy adult womanhood with its primary function being the reproduction of healthy children and for the maintenance of the race. Madame Bergman-Osterberg, while a progressive pioneer of increased female opportunity, left no doubt as to her eugenic sympathies. Her concern for the future teaching of physical education reiterated eugenic arguments about race regeneration:

> I try to train my girls to help raise their own sex, and so accelerate the progress of the race: for unless the women are strong, healthy, pure and true, how can the race progress? (quoted in May 1969: 52)

The development of physical education increased sporting and physical opportunities for women but their primary objective was healthy motherhood rather than personal liberation. As Katherine McCrone (1982) argues, the main intention of physical education was

> to preserve and improve women's health and thus heighten their chances of producing healthy children; it had nothing to do with freeing women from traditional restrictions or bodily movements. (McCrone 1982: 7)

Although physical education was constrained within the ideology of motherhood, opponents to women's increasing educational opportunities focused on physical education as a hazardous development in girls' schooling with the potential for overstrain and serious bodily damage. Dr Mary Scarlieb, writing in 1911, reflected this opinion:

> Doctors and schoolmistresses observe that excessive devotion to athletics and gymnastics tends to produce what may perhaps be called the 'neuter' type of girl – her figure, instead of developing a full feminine grace, remains childish – she is flat-chested with a badly developed bust, her hips are narrow and in too many instances there is a *corresponding failure of function*. (quoted in Dyhouse 1981: 130, emphasis added)

This view was supported by Dr Murray Leslie, who suggested that playing hockey might result in the inability to breastfeed in later life (Dyhouse 1976: 46), and by Arabella Kenealy, who argued strongly against the physical and mental exercise of girls, which she professed would result in 'sex extinction' (Kenealy 1920). Even some of the original supporters of secondary schooling for girls expressed concern about these developments in physical activity. Sara Burstall, herself a product of the 'new' high schools and later to become headmistress of Manchester High School, wrote:

> Important as are bodily vigour and active strength . . . in the men of a country who may have to endure the supreme test of physical fitness in war the vitality and passive strength – potential energy – of its women are even more important, since Nature has ordained women to be the mothers of the race. (Burstall 1907: 90)

The relationship between physical education and health, and the continuous concern for the development of healthy womanhood (i.e. healthy motherhood), was fundamental to the development of a systematic, comprehensive physical education programme. The opposition to physical activity and the potential damage it could do to women was not the prerogative only of outspoken individuals. It was legitimized and institutionalized by the formal incorporation of medical supervision and inspection into the everyday organization of physical education in the schools. While physical education developed as a progressive movement which increased women's physical opportunities, this was achieved within the boundaries of medical concern for women's future health. Girls were encouraged to become more physically active in order to promote good health and remedy weakness or physical deformity. However, behind these progressive moves was a primary concern to prevent damage to their reproductive organs and to protect and guarantee their future role as mothers. The adoption of limited and adapted games not only reinforced an ideology of femininity but also was premised on an ideology of motherhood. The pioneers of physical education were careful to tread a fine line between gradually increasing physical freedom without challenging the biologically determined assumptions of women's primary function in life – motherhood. Woman-as-mother also was fundamental to the ethos of physical education training in the new teacher training colleges. The physical education colleges encouraged an atmosphere of family life with the principal as 'mother' shepherding her flock. As Sheila Fletcher (1984) discovered, when researching the history of Bedford College:

> The family spirit, even at the start with only thirteen students, was at least as much a reflection of attitudes as it was of numbers. (Fletcher 1984: 59)

A system of college 'mothers' was instigated throughout all the colleges, whereby older students 'mothered' the new intake of first-year students. As Sheila Fletcher (1984: 69) reflects: 'Generations of students were lapped up in this warm amniotic fluid'. Thus the ideology of motherhood was as deeply rooted in the ethos of physical training as it was in the development of physical activity for girls. The combination of these two factors resulted in secondary school girls receiving a physical education curriculum underpinned by institutionalized assumptions about their primary function and future role as mothers.

Sexuality

From the earliest years of physical education in high schools there was a well-established commitment to the moral connotations of physical education. As the headmistress of Sheffield High School reported in 1898: 'moral effects are of greater importance than any increase of measurement or of muscular vigour' (*Special Reports on Educational Subjects* 1898: 133). This was reiterated by her colleague Penelope Lawrence at Roedean, who considered the 'moral influence of physical education for girls is of great value' (ibid: 145).

What was meant by morality encompassed all forms of exemplary behaviour and standards concerned with appearance, discipline, conduct, clothing and social graces. Above all they were expected to demonstrate respectability through their behaviour and demeanour. During the period when physical education laid its foundations female sexuality was seen to require 'responsibility' and 'protection'. Women's sexuality needed regulation if women were to fulfil, successfully, their future female role. Sheila Fletcher (1984) describes the training of physical education teachers in the early colleges as a 'Peter Pan world' that was both long and sexless. The creation of this 'sexless' world was important because of the fear of lesbianism in an all-female environment. The denial of sexuality was consciously made to protect against criticisms that female physical education teachers may not be 'real women'. This *supposedly* sexless world is significant for it was the values developed through teacher training which filtered into the teaching of physical education in secondary schools. Both Colin Crunden (1974) and Sheila Fletcher (1984), in their histories of Anstey College and Bedford College, report an emphasis on 'petty' discipline in an atmosphere often described by past students as a convent or a nunnery. The 'sexless' world of physical education training in early years involved no contact with the opposite sex, no male visitors and a general emphasis on morality and modesty. Modesty was an essential aspect of femininity – the desirable behaviour and attitude of 'young ladies'. At the turn of the century ideal femininity was synonymous with female sexuality. Ideally, women's sexuality was hidden or denied and the training of physical education teachers stressed a particular ideology of female sexuality in both its 'formal' curriculum and the 'hidden', underlying ethos of the courses.

An improvement in 'mind and character' was developed through the encouragement of 'standards' of discipline, neatness, self-control, respect for authority, dedication and service to others. In 1905 the *Anstey College of Physical Training Magazine* reported that the main aims of physical training included

> Regular attendance, good behaviour throughout the year, and general improvement in all respects. Smart personal appearance shown by general care of the body as regards hair, teeth, skin, nails, clothing and good health.
>
> Good posture when standing and sitting and good carriage when walking. Attention to word of command, absence of mistakes and

vigorous work in the gymnasium. General forms and style of movement, sense of time, self-control and power of relaxation. (Crunden
1974: 19)

Swedish gymnastics, with its emphasis on 'precision smartness'
(Lawrence 1898), provided the perfect activity to encourage these
'standards'. Gymnastics encouraged increased moral consciousness
and health through its emphasis on remedial and therapeutic work.
A notion of 'service' to others was implicit and training involved
work in local clinics, orphanages and, at Anstey, the taking of
classes at public elementary schools. Future teachers of physical
education, therefore, were encouraged into the role of 'helper'. They
were learning to service others, just as in later life they would service
husband and children. Interestingly games playing, both in the colleges and in the high schools, encouraged a similar servicing role.
Whereas the boys of the public schools and grammar schools were
being taught leadership qualities through character-building exercises on the playing fields, girls were encouraged into team games to
develop a moral consciousness relating to the unquestioned discipline of rules and regulations.

Penelope Lawrence (1898) considered games as 'more satisfactory
than any other exercise'. Their importance lay in their ability to
train character and thus involved an education 'in obedience to law
and in acting together to a common end'. In contrast, young men
were encouraged into games 'to make a man of you' (Springhall
1985). Leadership, dominance and decision-making were promoted
on the rugby pitch and cricket field. Games playing was directly
associated with the development of masculinity, and adult masculinity was intrinsically associated with mature male sexuality.
Boys needed to develop a form of sexuality involving activity, ini-
tiative and control in order to develop into acceptable manhood.
For girls sexually appropriate behaviour involved modesty, passivity and responsibility. While team games allowed for energetic
activity, they were controlled by the restricted direct contact with
other players or the hockey/lacrosse ball. These games were acceptable because there was an implement between the ball and the
player. Physical contact was taboo on the playing field and within
the gymnasium. Netball, while allowing contact with the ball, was
adapted for girls in its restriction of space, reduction in speed and
avoidance of physical contact.

In all activities girls' bodies are extended and constrained in this
choreography of their future which they learn unconsciously in legs,
arms, hands, feet and torso. (Okeley 1979: 132)

The need to 'protect' women, not only for their future reproductive
function but also from any hint of sexual contact or sexual awareness, was paramount. They were responsible for maintaining
modesty and the connections between childhood, femininity and
asexuality were supported by physical education. The opposition to
girls playing team games was linked directly to the concern that it
would affect their development into ideal femininity and moral
womanhood. The image of women faced two directions – 'the vir-
gin or the whore' (Jackson 1982). By undertaking 'masculine' pursuits young women would be in danger of developing 'masculinity'
and an 'active' sexuality. Thus the pioneers of physical education
trod the new path to physical activity with restraint. At no time did
they challenge the ideology of women's sexuality and they were
careful to adapt and encourage new physical pursuits which could
incorporate this ideology and contribute to its reproduction.

The existence of limitations to the new-found freedom of physical
exercise, imposed by assumptions around young women's developing sexuality, was most apparent in the reforms in women's dress
and clothing which took place at the turn of the century. Physical
education contributed to these innovations by the development of
the gymslip and tunic which allowed for greater freedom of movement than previously had been considered socially acceptable or
sexually appropriate. Yet these changes retained an emphasis on
modesty and carefully masked any hint of the developing sexuality
of young women. As Judith Okeley (1979) reports:

> our bodies were invisible, anaesthetized and protected for one man's
> intrusion later. As female flesh and curves, we were concealed by the
> uniform. Take the traditional gymslip – a barrel shape with deep
> pleats designed to hide breasts, waist, hips and buttocks, giving free-
> dom of movement without contour. (Okeley 1979: 131)

Morality and modesty – sexually appropriate behaviour –
remained the firm responsibility of girls and young women through
their appearance and behaviour. Physical education, although
liberating women from many bodily restrictions and conventions of
dress, was careful to protect the sexuality of young women with a
reaffirmation of 'feminine' modesty and 'desirable' dignity.

From this excursion into the history of the origins of physical education it is apparent that ideologies of femininity, motherhood and sexuality underpinned the development of physical education and became integrated into its traditions and practice. It is important to recognize that the development of physical education in secondary schools for girls was not simply a progressive movement which contributed to women's increased access to physical activity and the experience of freedom of movement. Its development did not occur in isolation but reflected the social, political and economic position of women in the late nineteenth and early twentieth centuries. It was part of a move towards increased educational opportunities for women and the demand for more sport and leisure opportunities. However, ideologies about women's ability, role and behaviour became institutionalized within the physical education profession. Consequently secondary school girls experienced a subject which contributed to their liberation in terms of dress, opportunities for physical activity and access to a future profession, yet reaffirmed clear physical sex differences, their future role as mothers and the boundaries and limitations of women's sexuality. Furthermore, working-class girls had to wait many years before they experienced similar opportunities. It was the nineteenth-century legacy, derived in the elitist, middle-class schools, which provided the basis for the comprehensive system of girls' physical education which was central to the tripartite system of schooling in the post-1944 era.

It is important to consider the significance and extent of this legacy in relation to gender ideologies, by tracing the developments in physical education from these early beginnings to the present day. Through necessity this section will provide only a schematic commentary on the detailed history of contemporary physical education.

Physical education in the post-1918 era

By the end of the First World War physical education in the new secondary schools for middle-class girls had undergone approximately fifty years of development. It had reached the stage where an increasing number of secondary high schools included a comprehensive system of physical education in their curricula and the teacher training colleges were flourishing. The circle was reaching out further as more trained teachers entered the schools, encouraged physical education development and initiated the progression of more secondary pupils along the path towards teaching. Yet this progression in physical education and women's sport received considerable resistance and opposition. In 1920 Dr Arabella Kenealy published her book, *Feminism and Sex Extinction*, in which she spelled out the damaging effects of strenuous pursuits such as hockey on the feminine image and on women's capacity to feed their future offspring! The 1922 *British Medical Journal* report, *The Education of Girls*, was not so heavily opposed to physical education for young women but was careful to warn that

> games and sport tend to foster a love of pleasure detrimental to home and other interests, and to lessen womanly qualities . . . injurious effects may come from injudicious exercising on gymnastic apparatus. (*British Medical Journal* 1922: 11)

The general mood among physical educationalists, however, was positive and their developments continued within a framework which was tempered so as not to antagonize or challenge the 'medical' position too directly. A new textbook on *Gymnastics for Women*, written by Braae Hansen, a lecturer at the College of Hygiene and PE, Dunfermline, was reviewed in the *Journal of Scientific Physical Training* at this time. This text reflected the continuing acceptance of inherent physical sex differences to be heeded in the teaching of girls:

> there are a fair number of teachers who maintain that gymnastics for men and gymnastics for women can and should be conducted along the same lines, with the modification, that as women are muscularly weaker than men, their exercises should be less vigorous. Such teachers are far behind – many differences are inborn . . . any attempt to minimize them, would not be beneficial to the individual or the race. (*Journal of Scientific Physical Training*, vol. XI, 1918–19)

The suggestions for 'suitable' gymnastics for women included the 'avoidance of too sudden vigorous exertions' with gymnastics keeping 'the feminine form of movement not sharp or marked'. This emphasis on 'suitable' exercises for women was reflected in a positive review of a new book in a later edition of the *Journal of Scientific Physical Training* (vol. XII, 1919–20). The article praised a

publication by Max Parnet (1920) – *Woman her Health and Beauty*.
Its main strength was that it had 'drawn up a series of movements
easy to understand, suitable for home performance and aiming at
the acquirement of health and beauty'. Obviously these three
attributes were extremely desirable for women's physical leisure
activities!

During the 1920s the therapeutic and remedial nature of physical
education, which had gained momentum from the war years, was
emphasized when the necessity for massage and rehabilitation from
the hospitals had provided an obvious objective for women's physical education colleges. The stress on medical gymnastics was
apparent in an advertisement for Liverpool Training College published in 1927. The advertisement included the following details:

- Provides a professional training for the education of women in
  remedial and educational gymnastics.
- Games (hockey, lacrosse, tennis, badminton, rounders, cricket).
- Recreational and Rhythmic Exercise.
- Dancing (Rhythmical, Classical, Operatic, Folk and Social).
- Swimming – Fencing – Rowing, Girl Guide Work.
- Theory, Anatomy, Physiology, Hygiene – Massage – Medical,
  Electrical, Anatomical.

> (*Journal of Scientific Physical Training*, vol. XIX, 1926–27)

In the late 1920s the major change in physical education was the
gradual move away from the Ling system of exercise. This development occurred mainly through the work of Eli Bjorksten, who
encouraged more rhythmical gymnastics with the use of music.
Although her main text, *Principles of Gymnastics for Women and
Girls*, was published originally in 1918 it was not until the trans-
lated, revised edition appeared in 1932 that the full impact of her
work was felt. Advocates of this system had begun to develop work
in the colleges during the 1920s but the developments filtered
through to the schools in the early years of the 1930s. The most
striking feature of this new gymnastics was the continued concern
for women's 'natural' predispositions. The book provides a wealth
of information concerning 'excessive strain' or 'damaging' movement. It warned against 'ungainly' movement and suggests that 'the
wish for beauty in gymnastics is one worth gratifying' (Bjorksten
1932: 44). It went to considerable length to explain the physical
inferiorities and weaknesses of women, finally concluding:

> In a comprehensive review of the most noticeable differences in phy-
> sique between men and women we find that *women are, in almost
> every respect inferior.* Disregarding the fact – which may be taken
> for granted – that this difference is in accordance with the purposes
> of nature, we who have to develop women's gymnastics must start
> from existing conditions. A *woman's more delicate physique requires
> appropriate exercises.* There must be no attempt at training a muscu-
> lar power which is quite disproportionate to her capacity, no exer-
> cises which are harmful to her body and alien to her mental tendency
> . . . Womanliness in the real meaning of the term must not be lost
> sight of in gymnastics, *the aim of which should be to form a type of
> woman who, more than has ever been the case, before in civilized
> societies, is able to fulfil her own special function – motherhood.*
> (Bjorksten 1932: 142, emphases added)

The transition to more rhythmical gymnastics, therefore, did little
to challenge assumptions around gender. Indeed, the main advocates of rhythmical gymnastics, clearly following Bjorksten's directions, based their activities on an acceptance of biological inferiority
and difference, and on the need to guarantee women's future mothering role.

In the inter-war years physical education was consolidated as a
comprehensive subject including gymnastics (both Swedish and
rhythmical), outdoor games, some dance, and swimming. It
remained predominantly a subject for the privileged schools of the
middle classes although educational opportunities for the working
class expanded slowly. Physical education remained a 'two nations'
system (Fletcher 1984) with some of the innovatory work spreading
to the developing senior schools of the elementary system.

This commitment to increased physical education within state
education gained momentum immediately after the First World War
when there was a national concern for the physical fitness of the
younger generation. For girls the eugenic overtones of such a concern remained dominant, as their fitness was concerned primarily
with ensuring the health of the future generation. One of the major
practical effects of this emphasis was the forging of more direct links
between the medical profession and school physical education. This
took the form of medical inspection in the schools with the Board of
Education report on physical education each year coming from the
Chief Medical Officer within his overall report on *The Health of the
School Child.* In addition, a system of physical education organizers

was introduced. Their function was to liaise between schools and local education authorities and to organize courses, day schools and summer camps in physical education activities with 222 employed to cover 169 local education authorities (Board of Education Report 1936). These organizers were drawn from the specialist teacher training colleges and on this basis the ethos and teaching of physical education, which had developed in the privileged high schools and public schools, gradually was extended to the state system of education. However, the gap between the 'two nations' remained significant. Even with the increased enthusiasm for secondary education for all children, opportunities for older girls remained limited and physical education remained restricted by lack of facilities and trained teachers.

Therefore, between the wars physical education continued to be the privilege of the middle classes, with some move to develop it in state schools. What is clear is that the physical education towards which these schools were moving, was the system developed during the nineteenth century and it was these traditions which were transferred to the teaching of all girls in the 1950s, as 'Secondary Education for All' became available. Where facilities remained limited, for example in city schools with playing fields unavailable, the games adopted were those requiring playground space only. Therefore, a 'two nations' system continued in relation to some of the activities pursued. However, the attitudes and ideas underlying the formation of these activities remained the same as those underlying the development of the middle-class sports for women and girls. Ideologies of gender were integral to the development of physical education in the original high schools and these ideologies were replicated as physical education became a more acceptable and available subject for all girls in secondary schooling.

Physical education after 1944

Post-war England and Wales experienced considerable educational and social change, particularly for women. The post-war years brought a 're-evaluation of the benefits of family life' with the 'central role of the mother as child-rearer and housekeeper' (Smart 1984: 49). The ideology of the family carried an emphasis on the relationship between mother and child and the importance of socialization and family life. The Beveridge Report (1942) and Beveridge (1948) reasserted women's role as voluntary carers within the family within the framework of welfarism. This concern for the family reflected the disruption caused in the wartime period. The family as a unit was identified as the primary stabilizing influence on society. As with the years following the First World War, there was anxiety over a falling birthrate and the need to replace the population losses. The baby-boom of the late 1940s guaranteed that women were returned to a mothering role. Elizabeth Wilson (1980) suggests:

> Universal free education for the young adolescent created an opportunity to educate young girls for their future role as wives and mothers. (Wilson 1980: 33)

Newsom (1948) epitomized the prevailing attitude which viewed women as biologically different from but equal to men. This ethos stressed the importance of 'feminine' and motherly virtues to be lauded and encouraged as important values to the advancement of society:

> The future of women's education lies not in attempting to iron out their differences from men, to reduce them to neuters, but to teach girls how to grow into women and to relearn the graces which so many have forgotten in the last thirty years. (Newsom 1948: 109)

During the 1950s and 1960s there was a continuing emphasis on child-centred learning, which for girls meant the centring of attention on their 'natural' attributes and their future roles as wives and mothers. Where they were prepared for work, it was a female-specific world reflecting a clear sexual division of labour.

During the post-war period physical education underwent several major changes, including a major break with tradition as Ling's Swedish system was finally replaced by a new approach to teaching gymnastics. Laban's movement approach took the female physical education world by storm and by the late 1950s modern educational gymnastics and modern educational dance were well established throughout Britain. No longer were these initiatives directed solely towards a middle-class elite, as an expanded teacher training system, with the introduction of 'wing' colleges (where PE was either a main subject with one other, or a second subject), ensured more in-depth physical education training for teachers entering all sections of the tripartite school system. This shift to a framework incorporating Laban's techniques fitted perfectly into the broader educational ideals of the time and the prevalent assumptions concerning girls' schooling. Just as Ling presented inherent ideals of womanliness in his system of exercise, so Laban stressed creativity, co-operation, unity and aesthetic discovery. As male physical education moved closer towards scientific inquiry around anatomical and physiological questions and an enthusiasm for circuit training and competitive games, women's physical education reaffirmed and celebrated 'feminine' qualities. Although competitive games remained at the forefront, movement principles were used for skill learning in team games. These were based on learning-by-discovery with shared experiences emphasizing co-operative play.

The 'different but equal' ethos prevalent in girls' schooling was reflected in the continued separation of physical education even in mixed secondary school contexts. The requirement of girls' physical education was seen to be different from that of boys, reflecting assumptions about different 'natural' abilities and interests. The developments in women's physical education reflected a distinctive and contrasting attitude by the female physical education profession towards competition and a scientific approach to movement. Whereas pre-war physical training had utilized scientific elements to develop a therapeutic and remedial approach, stressing posture and appearance together with caring qualities, the post-war scientific inquiry was seen to be more 'masculine' in approach, concentrating on tests, measurements, skill acquisition, and so on. Sports science, as a subject, eventually emerged from this scientific approach adopted by male physical educationalists. Female physical education distanced itself from these developments and remained faithful to its movement principles.

During the late 1960s and 1970s the process of comprehensivization spread throughout England and Wales. A policy of 'equality of opportunity' was adopted in the 1960s as concerns over class inequalities within education drew from the academic debates of the new sociology of education. Flexibility, variety and innovation became the watchwords of education with the launching of the Nuffield Foundation (1962), the Schools Council (1964) and numerous projects designed for mixed ability teaching and more 'progressive' approaches to learning. Yet throughout this period 'equality of opportunity' was concerned primarily with issues of class, other groups in society, such as women and ethnic groups, were given little attention.

In theoretical terms during the 1970s there was a change in emphasis as the economic recession closed in on educational expansion and women's politics made its presence felt. The 1975 Sex Discrimination Act made it unlawful to discriminate in terms of sex (although some facilities were exempt from the Act, e.g. sports clubs) and women began to question the school system in relation to gender differentiation and the reinforcement of ideologies of gender.

Throughout this period the major development in physical education was the introduction of options. They emerged during the 1970s for the upper years of secondary schooling, partly as a response to the raising of the school leaving age to 16 years, and partly due to a renewed interest in the connection between physical education and future leisure participation. Physical education continued to be taught, almost exclusively, to single-sex groups and it was not until the 1980s that questions relating to mixed versus single-sex physical education began to be seriously considered. Perhaps the most significant changes have been as a response to the 1988 Education Reform Act with the phasing in of a National Curriculum, increasing centralized control of education and local management of schools (LMS) (Flintoff 1990). Physical education is a 'foundation subject' within the National Curriculum but Anne Flintoff is sceptical about the potential for providing equal opportunities in physical education within the framework of the National Curriculum guidelines. She states:

> I am still pessimistic in terms of PE and its scope for providing a positive educational experience for all children, for a closer look at this work reveals that equal opportunities issues have been largely ignored and the hegemony of male, middle class and white values that underpin PE [have been] left unchallenged. (Flintoff 1990: 91)

Gender equality has been virtually ignored by the Education Reform Act. In physical education a major issue is whether equality of opportunity can remain on an agenda which is increasingly preoccupied with protecting its future within a compulsory core curriculum. Gender inequalities, as this chapter has indicated, are a fundamental part of the traditions, teaching and philosophy of physical education. For the future it is important that any critical feminist work in schooling that has developed in the 1970s and 1980s is utilized to inform policies, priorities and practices. In physical education, the research discussed in the following chapters, contributes to these feminist debates. The National Curriculum *is* an opportunity to reassess aims, objectives, content and evaluation. As Anne Flintoff comments:

> The implementation of the National Curriculum has opened up whole new avenues and opportunities for collaboration between PE teachers, lecturers and those involved in the wider remit of sport. What we need to do is use these opportunities to our advantage, and to make sure that *all* our voices are heard, not just the loudest or the most powerful. (Flintoff 1990: 98)

The research which I undertook aimed to explore whether gender ideologies continue to underpin the teaching of girls' physical education. Anne Flintoff suggests that if the culture of physical education is to change then teacher education must produce critical reflexive teachers who can challenge the status quo rather than reproduce dominant gender relations informed by hegemonic masculinity (Connell 1989). As the following chapters show this remains a difficult but essential challenge for the future of physical education teaching.

CHAPTER 3

Images of Femininity in Contemporary Physical Education

Historically physical education has been premised on a commitment to 'separate and different' curricula for girls and boys in school. As suggested in Chapter 2, underpinning the provision for girls were assumptions around 'femininity' categorized into three main areas: physical ability/capacity, motherhood and sexuality. It was the intention of the research project to examine the extent to which such assumptions remain dominant in the attitudes and ideas currently held by those involved in the policies and practices of contemporary physical education. In order to do this the extensive definitions and justifications of 'good practice' given by teachers and the physical education adviser, and collated from the interview transcripts, were considered (see Appendix). It was important to determine whether ideologies of femininity remain the same in contemporary physical education or whether they have been challenged and altered to reflect a 'new' liberated image of women in the 1990s unfettered by gender assumptions.

Physical ability/capacity

The historical material identified clear biological and ideological justifications for a different and separate physical education curriculum for girls based on the assumption of innate physiological differences which resulted in specific female physical abilities and capacities. As recently as 1969 Paul Weiss, whose work formed a

core element on most teacher training courses and remains on the
reading list of many teacher education courses today, wrote:

> One way of dealing with these disparities between the athletic
> promise and achievement of men and women is to view women as
> truncated males. As such they can be permitted to engage in the same
> sports that men do . . . but in foreshortened versions . . . so far as
> excellence of performance depends mainly on the kind of muscles,
> bones, size, strength that one has, women can be dealt with as frac-
> tional men. (Weiss 1969: 215–16)

This powerful and confident statement about women's abilities (or
lack of them) raises several issues. First, women are viewed as
deviant males – as 'truncated males' or 'fractional men'. Furthermore, because Weiss claims that women are inferior in 'muscles,
bones, size and strength' the sports in which they participate need
to be adapted. According to Weiss there is little doubt as to where
the power, ability and control in sport lies. The fact that women
will be permitted (by men) to engage in the same sports places
power firmly and unequivocally in male control.

The structured research interviews with the two advisers for
physical education (female and male) provide evidence of agree-
ment with Weiss, that girls and boys have different and comple-
mentary physical abilities.

> Boys and girls offer each other different abilities and strengths
> therefore they can help and encourage each other. It is the same for
> the teachers. I think in some respects men tend to be by and large
> games players and teachers and possibly their expertise in terms of
> games and analyses might help girls understand games a bit more. I
> think women tend to be au fait and *naturally* adapted to style
> and rhythm of movement from the gymnastic point of view. I
> think women in respect of that can also help the boys. (Male
> adviser)
>
> A lot of people, myself included, feel that boys can give the girls
> much more daring, adventure, excitement and of course the girls can
> give grace, finish, those things they are better at. (Female adviser)

Although not viewing girls or women as 'truncated males' the
female adviser accepted that women are different in a range of physical areas and need, therefore, to play games and sports which suit
their capabilities.

> Let's face it, boys have far more strength, speed, daring. Women are much more the devious species. We need to play the games to suit our abilities. (Female adviser)

Out of the fifty-six interviews with those in a position of responsibility for decisions relating to the teaching of physical education in the authority (i.e. advisory staff, heads of department, peripatetic teaching staff) fifty-three referred to the existence of clear 'natural' sex differences. For example:

> Look at gymnastics, boys have no finesse but all little girls are poised. Little boys just throw themselves about.

> Boys and girls complement each other. They are different and we shouldn't be trying to make them the same. They can give to each other – girls' subtlety and control. Boys can stretch the girls and make them want to try harder.

> Very few girls are willing to launch themselves out of line . . . it's a physical difference. They've [boys] got spunk – girls naturally don't launch themselves.

> Boys are stronger, taller, faster. It's just a physical difference.

> I think boys are much more rowdier and noisier and therefore shouldn't be put with girls. It's just natural.

The interview transcripts suggest the existence of strong images and ideas about girls' and boys' physical capabilities. As can be seen from the above quotes, boys are viewed as

> daring, exciting, rowdy, noisy, boisterous, strong, tall, fast, spunky, willing to launch themselves.

In contrast girls are seen to possess

> finesse, poise, subtlety, control, grace, finish, quietness.

The explanations for the existence of these two distinct sets of male and female characteristics fall into two areas. First, there was reference by the majority of the teachers to *'natural'* differences which were accepted as biologically determined. Yet these powerful stereotypes held by the teachers are not supported so definitively by research evidence. Ken Dyer (1982) suggests that, in relation to sporting ability and physical capacity, physical sex differences are relevant only at the highest competitive level and even here it remains difficult to identify 'biological fact' from the social effects of socialization, training opportunities, and so on. Certainly, observation of physical education of 13-year-old girls in the case study schools suggests that there are as many physical differences in relation to physique, strength and co-ordination *within* the group as there are in comparison to a similar age group of boys.

Not all teachers placed their stereotypical perceptions within a biological framework. The second explanation identified *social tradition* and *cultural determination* as more significant in creating gender differences in physical ability and capacity. However, this did not reduce the inevitability of their assumptions. As one teacher commented:

> I think it is tradition but I'm part of that tradition and convention and I wouldn't want to or be able to change it.

These comments indicate that powerful attitudes remain which centre on girls' physical ability and capacity based on the assumption that girls are physically less capable than boys and, in general, exhibit specific 'female' or 'feminine' characteristics (e.g. poise, grace, control, finesse, sensitivity). Although the interviews indicated a divergence of opinion as to whether these differences are rooted in biology or culture, the emphasis remains on the *acceptance* of physical differences and the desirability to reproduce these differences through the teaching of physical education. Consequently, these ideas and images are used to justify the type of activity offered to girls and boys.

> We have just not got the fore-arm strength to play hockey like the boys. Changes in the rules are a disastrous development. Netball is the same – it is especially suitable for girls.

> I don't think boys would be satisfied doing netball. It's far too static a game for boys. They [boys] need more excitement and freedom.

Where a traditionally female activity, such as modern educational dance, was considered for boys, there was seen to be a need to adapt it to 'masculinity':

> Dance as a subject lends itself to girls but there is a place for boys as well even if fitness training to music or something like that.

> Dance is fine for boys so long as you use appropriate themes. They would need to do stronger, more assertive movements probably with a more dramatic element.

It was in the discussion of traditionally male activities, such as soccer and rugby, however, that the strongest views were expressed by the female physical education staff. While many teachers agreed that girls are capable of the physical skills to play soccer, the following quotes represent the strength of attitude against soccer as a desirable female activity.

> I have yet to see an elegant woman footballer. Maybe I'm just prejudiced but they look just horrible. I just don't like seeing women playing football. If they did I would definitely want to modify it. The pitch is far too big and the ball too hard. No, I certainly wouldn't ever want to see girls playing football.

> Football! – I have a personal thing about this. I've been to a woman's football match and there's nothing sorer to my feminine eyes than a big bust and a big behind and the attracted crowd and spectators. . .I won't let the girls play because it is very, very unfeminine – I associate that with a man. I feel very strongly that I will never let the girls play soccer.

It is not the biological constraints which deem football unsuitable for girls but the undesirability of it in relation to definitions of femininity. Football displays those qualities previously associated by the teachers with boys – noisy, fast, boisterous, with the need to launch themselves about the pitch. Therefore it is not seen as a suitable or desirable activity to be encouraged for girls in physical education. As one head of department commented:

> If girls want to go off and play football then they can go and play in a park or club. It is definitely not our place to encourage those activities in school times.

Soccer raised the strongest antagonism among the women teachers, primarily because it was acknowledged that girls can and do play soccer. Therefore the need to challenge any demand for its inclusion in the physical education timetable seemed necessary. Other 'masculine' pursuits such as rugby and boxing were dismissed by *all* the teachers as undesirable and unsuitable for girls.

> I'm too stereotyped to even think of women playing rugby.

> No way rugby – that's even more extreme than soccer. Apart from the physical contact it is also about tradition but in these cases it is definitely right. I think I'm a bit inflexible in my way of thinking.

The reasons for their opposition to 'masculine' pursuits rested on traditional assumptions about desirable 'feminine' behaviour and a concern about physical contact between girls. The issue of physical contact relates directly to the social construction of female sexuality and will be discussed later in this chapter. Overall the interview material suggests that common-sense assumptions and stereotypes concerning girls' and boys' 'natural' physical abilities and capabilities have significant consequences for the teaching of physical education and result in gender differentiated practices. The historical legacy, together with powerful contemporary common-sense assumptions, result in the institutionalization of gendered policies, priorities and practices.

Motherhood

> If there has to be some difference in the physical education of girls at school, this will need to concern the specifically female functions of their organism and to aim at countering the infirmities brought about by the unnatural life of women in the civilized world . . . From this point of view their physical education will need to be supplemented by exercises strengthening them in their specifically female role of childbearing. It should include training for motherhood. (Pantyazopoulou 1979: 1)

This view of the link between physical education and girls' preparation for their future role in motherhood relates back to the eugenics movement of the early twentieth century. Today there is little evidence that similar attitudes relating to motherhood are held by physical education teachers. Whereas historically, physical education was seen as health-related, ensuring the future well-being of the race, today health objectives tend to be concerned with encouraging and promoting an 'active lifestyle'. This does not deny the contemporary significance of the ideology of motherhood in determining women's central role, but government-funded health services, developments in techniques of childbirth and improved health care have diminished the assumed necessity for education to concentrate on this aspect of physical fitness. Having said that, many of the teachers interviewed discussed the perceived role of their students as wives and mothers:

> They'll all be married within a couple of years with a couple of kids to look after.

In this day and age most of the girls will have kids quite soon. With unemployment there's little alternative really.

The power of ideologies of motherhood and domesticity lie in their assumed inevitability for most girls and young women. In the teaching of physical education this has direct consequences for both female staff and their female pupils. Unique constraints on time are experienced by women, be they daughter, sister, wife or mother. The expectation is that it is the woman who undertakes the 'caring' role. Women physical education staff recognized the restrictions they experience, the consequences of which govern their own opportunities to offer comprehensive and detailed extra-curricular programmes. They were well aware from their experiences that the primary responsibility for collecting children, buying food, cooking dinner, cleaning and organizing the household lies with women.

It's okay for the men, they stay at school running the clubs, organizing teams until about 7 p.m. Go home and sit down to their meal and then relax, put their feet up or go for a drink so that they are refreshed for another day. We have to fit in the shopping etc. around our working day.

Domestic responsibilities were not experienced only by married women although a survey of the interviewees in this research showed that 55 per cent were married and of these 75 per cent had children. The remaining 45 per cent, however, also had domestic responsibilities, either for dependent relatives or on a shared basis with flat-mates. None of the female heads of department were free from the majority of domestic chores. There were indications also that women physical education staff increasingly are remaining in full-time employment after having children. Although there is no reliable statistical evidence for this, several heads of department with children commented that they had returned immediately after having children because of economic necessity rather than choice. When asked about this trend the female adviser agreed that

Women used to take time out to have a family but now they stay with maternity leave. That change is most noticeable over the past ten years.

Her analysis however, left no doubts as to where she saw women's primary responsibility once they had children:

It is good for a child to have their mother, or maybe their father, around the house. I can see that it is good for women with small children to have part-time jobs. In fact that is very important for the women and the children but it is wrong to have full-time work. It is only storing up problems for society.

Certainly the responsibility for organizing child-care remains with the woman. These societal expectations of women's role in child-care and domesticity have severe repercussions for the daily routine of female staff, in relation to time and commitment to extra-curricular teaching. Consequently this directly affects opportunities for participation by female school students. As a member of staff commented:

I would love to offer more things after school for girls and at the weekends but it is impossible. I have to pick up my little girl from nursery by 5 p.m. and then start on all the things that need doing at home. I just haven't got the time.

Similarly, young women students are often restricted by domestic and child-care 'duties':

there are girls who are unable to take part because of commitments at home – going to collect younger brothers and sisters. In some cases part-time jobs. I know that they feel that they have to do it while brothers don't – collecting children, making tea etc.

Boys don't have problems of staying. Some kids have to pick up younger kids from junior school etc. The girls do the messages don't they?

Lots of girls would stay but they have to pick up little brothers and sisters from school, get the family allowance etc. Boys don't have the same commitments.

Girls are the ones that do the laundry and household tasks. That is so obvious with women if you look at Sunday league football.

Ideologies of motherhood and domesticity no longer appear explicitly to influence the content and teaching of physical education. However, it is the dominance and internalization of these ideological constructions of the 'woman's place' which puts indirect, but substantial limitations, on physical education through restrictions on the experiences and opportunities afforded to both female staff and female students. Although physical education teachers no longer identify their central objective as being the preparation of physically fit young women for healthy motherhood, neither do they identify any need to challenge directly societal expectations that women's roles are those of wife and mother. Indeed, many still view this as women's natural function or, if not biologically determined, then culturally expected. Physical education does not overtly reinforce such expectations, but they remain implicitly on the hidden agenda of attitudes and ethos which underpin the curriculum.

Sexuality

Discipline, good behaviour and appearance, so much a part of the tradition and standards set by physical education in the pioneering girls' schools of the late nineteenth century, continue to be stressed today. Every head of department of girls' physical education throughout the local education authority studied identified the maintenance of 'standards' relating to dress, appearance, discipline and good behaviour as first or second in their priorities for teaching:

> I think there must be very high standards.

> Within PE departments girls can't get away with much. Standards are set quite high – we impose standards which other teachers may not impose.

> I think the standards in all the schools need to be high. I think PE people quite often have higher standards than a lot of people . . . we expect a higher standard of behaviour and attitude – loyalty almost.

The heads of girls' physical education, however, did not extend these priorities to the boys. As one teacher commented:

> I think we do stipulate more, trying to make them into 'young ladies'.

The emphasis on 'young ladies' implies a particular conception of 'standards' relating to both expectations of behaviour and appearance. Acceptable female behaviour involves restraint, quietness and orderliness.

> We are quite strict on discipline, for example we make sure the girls are orderly, lined up and ready for a lesson before they start.

The girls know that they go into the gym, find a space and sit down quietly. They know that's expected of them. If you watch the boys they just rush in and start climbing wall bars and things. We expect different things for the girls.

We spend a lot of time making sure the girls are in a quiet line before they even go into the gym or outside. I know it takes some time but those standards are important.

Iris Young (1980) argues that girls learn throughout childhood to protect their bodies and to inhabit a very limited personal body space. As a girl reaches adolescence she

learns actively to hamper her movements. She is told that she must be careful not to get hurt, not to get dirty, not to tear her clothes, that the things she desires to do are dangerous to her. Thus she develops a bodily timidity which increases with age. In assuming herself as a girl she takes herself up as fragile. (Young 1980: 153)

Restraint on movement is the outcome of the control and discipline seen by staff as essential for 'successful' girls' physical education. Although girls are encouraged to be physically active the teachers' comments suggest that the girls are not expected to be adventurous in their movements. 'Neatness', 'finish' and 'controlled movements' were constantly mentioned as 'female' characteristics. Furthermore (as mentioned in Chapter 2) the development of girls' sports was premised on such notions of 'femininity': netball with its restricted movement and use of space; hockey with close control with the stick and rules governing spatial movement.

It is feasible to conclude that the restrictions on the use of personal and physical space embodied in the rules of girls' sports, together with assumptions around the need to restrict and control girls' movements, encourage young women to learn that their bodies need protecting and that they must remain enclosed within personal space. Iris Young (1980: 153) emphasizes that in physical development girls 'acquire many subtle habits of feminine bodily comportment – walking like a girl, tilting her head like a girl etc.' While physical exercise and sport encourage a wider and explorative use of space, the activities offered and the attitudes held by many teachers reinforce a limited extension of this bodily use. She goes on to argue an interesting point:

To open her body in free activity and extension and bold outward directness is for a woman to invite objectification . . . She also lives the threat of invasion of her body space. The most extreme form of such spacial and bodily invasion is the threat of rape... I would suggest that the enclosed space which has been described as a modality of feminine spaciality is in part a defence against such invasion. (Young 1980: 154)

To an extent physical education teaching accepts the limitations and the responsibilities women have for their own protection. A feminist critique of physical education must develop an analysis of the politics of sexuality which defines women as vulnerable and, therefore, in need of protection. 'Standards' for girls centre also on expectations about appearance:

> We don't just teach the girls PE, we always include a lot of other bits and pieces e.g. hygiene, cleanliness, dressing well in PE kit, uniform.
>
> I teach them to have correct uniform, kit, hair tied back, attention to detail.

Even during lessons girls are encouraged to look good and discouraged from being boisterous. As one head of department summed up:

> The whole thing is dictated by the fact that there is a very female atmosphere in PE here and the look of the thing is as important as the doing it. It's not so for the boys – they look as scruffy going on to the rugby pitch as they do coming off it.

'Appearance' is central to female sexuality. Feminist literature on sexuality emphasizes that in their appearance women are defined in relation to sexual attractiveness but not sexual availability. The female body is defined and portrayed in a specific form geared to an 'ideal' image of femininity. Ros Coward (1984) argues:

> Because the female body is the main object of attention, it is on women's bodies or women's looks that prevailing sexual definitions are placed... The emphasis on women's looks becomes a crucial way in which society exercises control over women's sexuality. (Coward 1984: 77)

Certainly the heads of department placed considerable emphasis on appearance and defined it in terms of the stereotypical image of 'ideal' femininity. There is an assumption that young women should look good, be presentable and concern themselves with self-image. Historically, physical education, although liberating in its encouragement of increased physical activity and the breaking of some dress conventions, was careful to protect the sexuality of young women by a reaffirmation of 'feminine' modesty and 'desirable' dignity. The persistent emphasis by those concerned with the policies and practices of physical education, on standards of dress, appearance and behaviour, raises important questions about the relationship of physical education to ideologies of physicality and the politics of sexuality.

The issue of physical contact and its relationship to sexuality is an important aspect of gender relations and remains a central issue for teachers of girls' physical education.

> I don't see any place for rugby taught in school because of the contact.

> I think girls could probably try anything within reason. Girls shouldn't be doing weights and I don't think I'd put girls into rugby tackling for physical reasons. They could hurt themselves about the chest as they are tackling someone.

The argument does not hinge on a belief that violent contact sport might be considered unsuitable for all young people, but that 'contact' is not suitable for girls.

> I don't mind boys playing rugby but I don't think it's a girls' sport. It's like boxing really. They might enjoy it but I wouldn't enjoy seeing them battering each other.

Girls are seen as physically capable of playing the game but such behaviour does not befit a 'young lady'. Teachers interviewed, however, did not mind boys 'battering each other'.

> Well, it's different for boys, they enjoy it. I just don't think it would be particularly good for girls.

There appear to be two major objections to physical contact between women, both of which relate to female sexuality. The physical education adviser put forward the first argument with clarity:

> there is a physiological point. If we put adolescent girls into that situation I might be concerned about the damage they might do to their breasts with hard knocks. After all, hockey, although a tough game, there is an implement between yourself and the ball. You can protect yourself, it isn't bust to bust!

This is the same argument promoted in the late nineteenth century to justify the development of separate and 'suitable' games for girls. There is a concern here about female physical vulnerability. This concern is most intense in relation to the need to 'protect' areas of the body which have either a reproductive function or sexual meaning in our society. No one commented on the problem of potential injury to the face, arms, etc. but several of those interviewed were concerned that knocks might harm breasts or buttocks. Physical contact is viewed as undesirable in relation to assumed female vulnerability, which is inextricably linked to ideologies about female sexuality. Yet the vulnerability of women's bodies is a curious assertion given the location of male reproductive organs! As M. Ann Hall (1979) comments:

> We see man as the protector raging against contact sports for females on the grounds that they will irreparably damage, among other things, their naturally protected reproductive organs, whereas the fact that male genitals have to be protected is never considered problematic. (Hall 1979: 28)

M. Ann Hall also offers a second explanation that can be put forward to explain the objection to physical contact between women:

> For a woman to subdue another woman through physical force and bodily contact is categorically unacceptable, the innuendo sexual and the act considered unnatural. There exists an age old prohibition against aggressive physical contact between women. (Hall 1979: 25)

The acceptance of aggressive and violent physical contact between boys, girls, men or women is open to question. Yet there remains a double standard which limits the need for regulation solely to women's behaviour and activities. The demonstration of power and assertion between women seems unacceptable in relation to the social construction of female sexuality. Desirable female sexuality is presented as a passive, responsible, heterosexuality and the involvement of women in contact sports immediately raises doubts about the status of their sexuality. It is the *power* expressed through physical strength in contact sports, rather than actual physical touch, which is problematic. Indeed, girls and women express their emotion and sensitivity, acceptable female traits, through physical contact. Heterosexual relations are premised on unequal power relations between men and women, with women traditionally expected to take the subordinate, passive role (Coveney et al. 1984; Jeffries 1985). Contact sport between women places one partner in the oppressive dominant position, a situation untenable in 'acceptable' female sexuality. This disapproval by physical education staff of contact sports between girls cannot be seen simplistically as a concern about potential physical injury. It is a concern directed specifically towards young women and should be analysed in terms of ideas around 'acceptable' female sexuality. This centres on commonly held expectations of heterosexuality, involving key notions of passivity, vulnerability and subordination.

A further issue identified by many physical education teachers also can be related to assumptions about acceptable female sexuality. The majority of staff commented that many girls could not stay for extra curricular activities during the winter because of travelling home in the dark. Often it was parents who enforced such restrictions:

> From about November some girls can't stay to clubs or practices because they're not allowed to walk home in the dark.

> There is a big problem of darkness especially with first and second year girls.

> The main restriction on girls staying is darkness and the distance they have to travel home.

> There's a real problem with away matches because parents don't like them travelling across the city in the winter in the dark.

The main concern is the protection of girls from the dangers of sexual attack. Implicit here is the recognition of men's direct physical control and dominance over women which is clearly evident in the extent of physical or sexual attack or abuse and the fear associated with it. The idea that girls and women require protection after dark is a substantiated reality. Most women feel vulnerable at night and this has implications for young women's participation in both extra-curricular activities in school and during their leisure time.

The message in relation to female sexuality remains clearly articulated through physical education. Women's bodies are physically developed in order to look good and presentable (particularly to men), yet they must be protected from overdevelopment and physical contact in order to avoid 'unnatural' or 'unhealthy' touch and damage to 'delicate' parts. Thus the ideological construction of the 'ideal woman' is consolidated in contemporary physical education practice.

The evidence presented in this chapter suggests that there remain powerful assumptions around femininity in relation to physical ability/capacity, motherhood/domesticity and sexuality. However, these images are not static reassertions of a nineteenth-century view of femininity. They have changed and developed over time. Physical expectations of women's capabilities have shifted and accept that women are not physically restricted to the degree assumed at the turn of the twentieth century. There has been a gradual increase in women's opportunities to experience and compete in a wider variety of physical pursuits. Women physical education staff acknowledge this expansion in participation and consequently their expectations of girls' abilities have increased. However, underpinning this developing awareness remains a powerful reaffirmation of a 'femininity' which deems young women and women as weaker, less physically powerful, less aggressive than their male counterparts while retaining more grace, poise, finesse, flexibility and balance. The importance is not in the accuracy of these stereotypes (indeed many young women exhibit such qualities) or in the arguments concerning biological determination or cultural reproduction, but as Paul Willis (1982) contends:

> that to know, more exactly, why it is that women can muster only 90 per cent of a man's strength cannot help us to comprehend, explain or change the massive feeling in our society that a woman has no business flexing her muscles anyway. (Willis 1982: 119)

The research project confirms this latter statement in relation to girls' physical education. Women teachers stated clearly that a young woman has 'no business flexing her muscles'. There has been some move to accept that women can partake in physical activities and reach levels of physical capability previously thought impossible in the female sporting world. Yet there remain precise and articulated constraints which set the limits and boundaries beyond which young women should not attempt to move. Further, the research suggests that such images and attitudes relating to young women's physical abilities, motherhood/domesticity and sexuality are reflected across class locations (identified across different types of schools), applying to young women be they working class or middle class. However, the research does indicate the complexity of the interconnections between gender and class. For example ideas around domesticity and motherhood present young working-class women with greater direct constraints, including the burden of child-care and domestic chores from an early age. Dominant gender images and ideas remain powerful across class locations, although they may be experienced to different degrees by women from different classes. This research, which concentrates on gender, does not allow for a full consideration of racial differences. Within the study no distinctions emerged relating specifically to 'race' and images of femininity, although this is an area requiring more detailed consideration for future work.

CHAPTER 4

Images in Action: Gender Differentiation in Physical Education Practice

In order to identify the significance of *gender* in the teaching of girls' physical education various aspects of contemporary physical education needed to be investigated. Initially a survey of all the schools in the local education authority (LEA), through interviews with the heads of girls' physical education departments, provided evidence of the organization, staffing, facilities, aims and objectives and curriculum, of physical education across the LEA. This was followed by the period of observation in four selected case study schools (see Appendix). This chapter introduces some of the findings of this intensive investigation, in particular the identification of various processes and practices which potentially reinforce gender images and ideas. Stuart Hall (1982) in considering the concept of ideology states:

> ideas do not arise spontaneously from inside our individual heads or from the depths of our individual consciousness! Ideas exist outside us, in society; in the discourse we use, the institutions we live and work in, the way things are arranged. Ideology is a social process. (Hall 1982: 25)

This is an important statement for it is not enough simply to identify sexist attitudes of teachers and pupils (although as the previous chapter has shown, these do exist), if a full investigation of gender inequality is to be achieved.

As Stuart Hall succinctly states, ideologies do not arise sponta-
neously in the heads of individuals but they exist within and are
transmitted through the institutions of society (including schools),
their policies and their practices. If ideology was reduced simply
to individual attitudes then reform focusing on gender and physical
education would be straightforward: remove the individuals holding sexist assumptions from the schooling process (teachers and
pupils) and gender differences would disappear (i.e. the equal
opportunities approach). However, research and publications into
gender and schooling (Spender and Sarah 1980; Arnot and Weiner
1987; Weiner and Arnot 1987) suggest that it is the institutionalization of gender ideas and images which reinforces the means by
which gender differences come to be taken for granted. This process creates powerful gender ideologies which can be identified in
the policies, priorities and practices of schooling. The identification of ideology, however, does not address the extent to which
ideas and images are taken up and assimilated by girls in the
learning situation.

Organization

Grouping: the mixed v single-sex debate

The issue of mixed versus single-sex grouping in schools has been
and remains a significant feminist debate, with many feminists
arguing vehemently for separate provision for girls to prevent
them from 'losing out' in the learning situation. Yet in physical
education separate provision is the tradition although (as shown in
Chapter 2) it is a tradition underpinned by ideologies of gender
defining girls and women in relation to femininity and incorporating expectations and assumptions about physical ability/capacity,
motherhood/domesticity and sexuality. More recently there have
been moves to break this tradition by introducing co-educational
physical education. Although not a central focus of the research,
interesting material emerged concerning mixed-sex grouping in
physical education and whether it is a progressive move for
girls.

The organization of physical education throughout the research
LEA was predominantly in single-sex mixed ability grouping. Of
the nineteen mixed schools visited, all taught the majority of

lessons in single-sex classes. Above the third year there were considerable differences in organization relating to the content taught. Five of the nineteen schools retained single-sex grouping throughout the five years of compulsory secondary schooling and introduced mixed lessons only during the sixth form. The remainder introduced some mixed activities in the final year of compulsory schooling with eight schools opting for some mixed physical education in the fourth year upwards. Consequently, physical education for the lower age-range of secondary schooling was taught to single-sex groups with mixed-sex grouping becoming an issue only for girls over the age of 14.

The retention of single-sex physical education for the lower years of secondary schooling reflected the generally negative view that the women physical education teachers had about mixed-sex grouping. One head of department summed up her feelings:

> when first I came here the PE was separate. It was pretty horrific but it mainly needed general organization. Then we tried mixed games and that was worse. I used to have to lock myself in the gym with these bad boys – fifth formers – 'cos lads have a different set of standards. I think if it is going to be mixed it's got to be from the start but I certainly wouldn't want that.

However, one of the schools observed – Heyfield – was conducting an experimental scheme of mixed first-year dance. During the observation period, first-year classes were observed over a period of five weeks. The sessions appeared to work successfully with girls and boys taking part with enthusiasm. Throughout the period of observation the theme of 'Time' was used. This included the use of a short written piece as stimulus and music as accompaniment. Yet within this mixed-sex teaching situation sexual divisions continued to exist. As the dance developed over the weeks boys continued to work together and the dance became choreographed into boys' sections and girls' sections. Although these sections were of equivalent length and importance within the whole dance it was significant that the groupings were divided solely on the basis of sex. Yet, it was noted during the period of observation that the girls and boys were at different stages of physical development. Some of the girls had started to mature physically and were quite tall. All of the boys were pre-pubescent and many had a small physique. Possibly it would have been more valid to choreograph dance using size as a consideration rather than sex. The grouping of the girls and boys by sex was exacerbated further by the response of the pupils. When asked to work in pairs or threes they tended to be self-selective in sex groupings. There was no positive intervention by the teacher to regroup the girls and boys into mixed-sex groupings.

The importance of observing mixed-group teaching is highlighted by this situation and raises several important questions. Is mixed-sex grouping in theory, mixed-sex teaching in practice? Is organization alone sufficient or is positive intervention necessary in order to encourage girls and boys to work together? Observation of the fourth- and fifth-year option sessions confirmed the need to address these questions. The option activities were timetabled as mixed activities. In practice, however, girls opted primarily for badminton and basketball in mixed groups. A large proportion opted for 'keep-fit', which was chosen only by girls, with nine girls in the fifth year opting for 'health and beauty'. This course was run by the head of department and offered only to the girls. The justification for the health and beauty course was derived from the presumed need (as defined by the head of department) to offer activities which would attract and maintain the interests of fifth-year girls. They spent the session considering make-up, hair-style, 'beauty tips' and fashion. The emphasis was on appearance, not on physical health. It was significant that a relatively small number of girls opted for this session given that it was a positive attempt to provide the girls with 'what they want' (head of department).

Similar situations were observed in the mixed badminton sessions in the sports hall. The badminton was 'coached' by a male member of staff. Throughout the observation period, five classes were observed. On three occasions each game in each court (doubles) was single-sex: boys played boys and girls played girls. The only exceptions were the five remaining players (three girls and two boys) who played against each other. On two occasions one pair of boys opted to play against one pair of girls (or vice versa) although each of the other courts were single-sex. At no time was there an attempt by the member of staff to intervene and alter the organization. The sessions were pupil-led in that they organized themselves and were supervised primarily by the staff member who offered some comments of encouragement and help and made occasional disciplinary interventions. In the fourth and fifth year the only 'non-traditional' choice made by the girls was the decision by five girls on two occasions to join the soccer group. Although mixed in theory, in practice outdoor team games such as football and netball remained single sex. However, on the occasion when the girls first opted to join the soccer group the head of department's comment as they left the changing room summed up the underlying attitude to the girls playing soccer:

> Football, you must be mad – you should have been born a lad.

Although girls in theory and practice had the opportunity to participate in soccer, effectively it remained at the level of equal access. In terms of their experience they ran the gauntlet of comment before leaving the changing rooms. Having joined the soccer group they were integrated into a male soccer group with a male member of staff. These boys had received soccer coaching throughout their five years at secondary school and for a minimum four years at primary school. This was the first opportunity to play soccer offered to the girls in a formal school teaching situation. Observation of the lesson suggested that equality of access cannot be equated with equality of experience or equality of outcome. The girls were given the opportunity to participate but it was a situation in which their lack of coaching and experience resulted in peripheral, rather than central, participation in the game.

The issue of the integration of girls into traditional boys' activities, and the subsequent problems, had been discussed previously with the head of department. She stated:

> We do some football. We have done now and again but I wouldn't put the girls in against the boys unless they wanted to. They'd have a go but they couldn't physically compete against them. They'd enjoy playing traditional boys' games themselves – they'd enjoy it more. The boys wouldn't give them a touch of the ball unless they are very good. We've got some girls who are very good but the majority of girls are more reserved than boys.

This quote is revealing for a number of reasons. First, it highlights the gulf between stated policy and practice. The stated policy recognizes the problems of girls being integrated into boys' soccer solely on the basis of choice. However, in practice this was exactly what happened, with the only opportunity for girls' soccer being the opportunity of access to the boys' soccer group. Furthermore, the justifications of, and explanations for, girls finding mixed soccer a problem were based on physical differences: 'girls are more reserved', 'they couldn't physically compete'. There is an implicit expectation that this is a 'natural' state of affairs. Thus when some girls challenge this by taking part in soccer it is their 'womanhood' which is questioned: 'you should have been born a lad'.

At Rosehill School similar observations were made of mixed-sex teaching although, as with the majority of schools in the authority, it was co-educational only in the sixth form. A mixed group of trampolining was observed each week for a five-week period. The lesson appeared to run smoothly using two trampolines and non-participants as spotters. The girls and boys took part on equal terms and received the same tuition. The only obvious problem created by the mixed setting was the embarrassment experienced by two of the girls through wearing physical education skirts. While this highlighted the problems faced by girls in wearing short skirts for physical education it could have been remedied as the girls had the freedom to wear tracksuit bottoms. In practice what happened was that the girls in skirts spent more time and attention in holding down their skirts or keeping them tucked in than acquiring trampolining skills. This demonstrated clearly that skirts are inappropriate, especially in mixed activities, and place limitations on girls' concentration and skill acquisition. The young women were acutely conscious of their sexuality in this situation and were embarrassed and intent on 'protecting' their appearance and presentation of self. The young men reacted initially with laughs and comments between themselves (inaudible). However, after a few minutes several young men showed their impatience in that it was 'wasting good trampoline time'. One commented:

> For goodness sake we see you in the pool in a 'cossie', leave your skirt alone!

Observation at Rosehill reinforced the observations at Heyfield School that mixed physical education in theory is rarely mixed physical education in practice. Although the timetable allowed some young women the opportunity to participate in mixed activities few took advantage of the opportunity. Furthermore, the practice of co-educational physical education highlights the significance of gender *and* sexuality for the experiences of girls and young women in a mixed setting of physical activity. It is important to stress, therefore, that organizational structures do not necessarily result in radical changes in gender differentiation. Mixed-sex lessons can still produce single-sex grouping within a particular activity, and images of femininity and masculinity can be reinforced independent of the grouping arrangements.

Attendance

Throughout the city schools, physical education was compulsory to the age of 16, in line with compulsory schooling. Approximately one-third of the schools continued compulsory physical education into the sixth form although some doubts were raised as to the success of the implementation of compulsion for this age group. Attendance at physical education lessons, however, was a major issue in all the case study schools observed. At Heyfield School, although physical education was compulsory up to and including the fifth year, it was noted that attendance fell after the third year. By the fifth year absenteeism from timetabled lessons was as high as 60 per cent. Although in most schools there was a satisfactory amount of time allocated to physical education, in practice the *experience* of physical education was often different. It was recorded throughout the fieldwork that a considerable amount of time was lost to physical education teaching through controversies over kit. Every lesson involved a minimum of three to five minutes discussion and checking of physical education kit. This did not necessarily involve enforcing schedules governing the correct kit; rather it was concerned with ensuring that as many pupils as possible changed into some form of alternative clothing or at least removed skirts, shoes and socks. Further time was lost in the removal of jewellery and the organization of hair. In timing the physical education lessons over a three-day period, on average sixteen minutes were spent at the beginning of each lesson in changing, sorting out kit, jewellery and hair. This was more than a quarter of the whole teaching time. Between eight and ten minutes were left at the end of each class for changing back into school uniform thus resulting in a loss of almost 50 per cent (average) of teaching time. Thus, although a set amount of time was allocated for physical education, absenteeism and issues relating to uniform created a situation in practice where many girls received a minimal amount of taught physical education each week.

The other schools observed did not spend so much time in enforcing the correct physical education uniform. At Rosehill School, however, the 'rules' and routines of physical education which involved lining up in silence in the changing rooms before moving to the lesson, meant considerably more time taken up with organization rather than with uniform. This routine was enforced with all groups from the first year to the fourth. With one group of third years and one group of fourth years it resulted twice in the lesson being missed. Furthermore, while leaving the changing room, comments from the staff stressed the girls' appearance and posture:

> Stand up straight.
>
> Stop leaning on the wall and stand straight.
>
> You look really scruffy: tie your hair back more neatly.

This emphasis on discipline, quite obvious in practice, was reiterated further by the head of department:

> We're more disciplined than any other part of the school. Girls respect us for it.

Archway School provided an interesting comparison as it was a middle-class single-sex Anglican school. Discipline and 'standards' of behaviour were not obvious problems.

It is interesting to question the relationship between gender and class. In *all* the case study schools a certain expectation of behaviour relating specifically to stereotypes of gender was observed. The lack of resistance to the enforcement of discipline in Archway School reflected a class response to a middle-class institution, with expectations which seemed more acceptable to the girls and not in conflict with expectations they received outside the school. Katherine Clarricoates (1980) argues, from her research in primary schools, that there are ideologies of femininity but that these are reflected and experienced differently in different class locations. Historically, physical education developed within middle-class schools originally for the daughters of the middle classes. The location of contemporary physical education remains within this historical context and the ethos and values relating to expectations of middle-class femininity continue to underpin the training of teachers and teaching in secondary school physical education. For the girls and young women at Archway School this did not contradict their experiences with their peers, family and, especially in this situation, their religion. It is likely that the girls and young women of Heyfield School sometimes experienced contradictory expectations, thus perhaps explaining their greater resistance to their experiences.

Staffing

The major issue concerning staffing related to extra-curricular school work. Of the schools surveyed only nine received any assistance from non-PE staff in out-of-school activities. This was commented on by every head of department interviewed and in the co-educational schools a direct comparison was made with the boys' physical education departments:

> We have one woman who does badminton whereas the boys have five members of staff who help with soccer teams.

> There is no help from other members of staff. The men do and we don't. Never have done. I run five netball teams by myself and it's really hard going.

> Help from other staff? – No! Mind you the boys get a lot of help with teams.

> Help – the men's department does but not the women's. There isn't anybody competent in taking teams. Men help with basketball and soccer teams. There are a number of men in school who are no longer teaching PE but were PE teachers or did PE as their second subject in college.

> No, we don't get any help. They come here and at interviews they promise the earth, they're going to run teams, etc. but when the time comes . . . The men run eleven soccer teams. With the men they all fancy being soccer managers. They even run staff teams for the men, there are that many interested.

The lack of extra-curricular teaching support in girls' physical education raises important issues about restricted opportunities to participate, the lack of correspondence between girls' physical education and female staff's leisure/sport interests, the lower profile of girls' physical activity in comparison to the high profile of boys' extra-curricular activities and sports, and the pressures on the time and abilities of female PE staff to have to teach all extra-curricular activities.

It is important also to note the number of years served by the teachers in the schools. The average was eight years, which is a considerable amount of time for an all-female profession traditionally serviced by women in their twenties or early thirties. The explanation for this was suggested by the following observations from physical education teachers:

> The turnover of staff is nowhere near as much as it used to be so we have less new, enthusiastic teachers entering. This has happened since 1974–1975 when the job situation became more difficult. Women are more likely to stay on when they have kids and just take maternity leave. They can't afford to give up their jobs anymore.

> Women used to take time out to have a family but now they stay and take maternity leave. There has been far less movement of staff in and out of the authority in the past ten years or so. People couldn't move even if they wanted to because there aren't the openings for promotion any more. If staff have reached head of department they are staying put.

During the period of the research physical education reflected the national situation in teaching with economic recession and educational cut-backs diminishing job opportunities and creating a static job market. This was confirmed by Flanagan HMI, the Staff Inspector for PE and Dance. In his opening address at the 1985 British Association of Advisers and Lecturers in Physical Education (BAALPE) Congress he commented that since 1977

> falling school rolls, a lack of movement, and restricted avenues for promotion have made for a smaller force, an older force and individuals staying longer in the same posts.

In relation to gender and girls' physical education the implications of such staffing changes include the following.

1 Innovations at teacher training level (e.g. equal opportunities) take longer to permeate through to the schools as staffing remains static.
2 As women remain longer in a post, their personal responsibilities often become greater. Thus an increased number of married women and mothers in the profession can lead to constraints on

time as women's dual role in the labour market and in the domestic and child-care situations becomes more intensified. This is the case especially in physical education where extra-curricular work is so important.
3 Fewer promotional prospects in relation to status and pay levels can result in more disillusionment and less willingness to undertake extra-curricular duties.

Facilities

All the schools in the authority had the basic amenities of a gymnasium and an outside hard-surface playing area. However, the limited number of schools having swimming pools and sports centres on site also affected the breadth and diversity of the activities on offer to the girls in physical education. Schools without swimming pools could offer only limited opportunities for teaching swimming. Twenty-one schools included swimming but only as a minor portion of the total physical education time. In secondary schools the teaching of swimming tends to be restricted to the first years, as financial priority is given to primary schools and lower secondary classes. Leisure research (Deem 1986) indicates that swimming is the most popular post-school leisure activity for women. Given that one of the primary aims of physical education teaching was identified by the teaching staff as 'preparation for leisure' (this is discussed later in this chapter) the lack of swimming facilities were clearly problematic in providing for the realization of this aim, thus denying inclusion of one main activity meaningful and relevant to young women's lives.

Adequate indoor facilities were seen by physical education teachers as essential in order to provide a satisfactory programme in poor weather conditions. Interestingly, this raises the question of what constitutes poor weather conditions for girls. On the whole, wet, cold, muddy fields were not seen by teachers to be suitable for girls' activities:

> We never got out in the rain, ice or fog. If it's very cold I only go out if we're doing something very active. There's no point in making it a punishment.

> Girls just won't go out once it's cold. If they do they just stand around and complain.

> Once the fields are muddy it just isn't worth taking the girls out.
> They complain and no one achieves anything.

While these comments reflect a fairly rational approach to a situation in which adverse weather conditions clearly affect the participation in and achievement of physical objectives, similar views were not expressed in relation to boys' experiences.

> Oh, boys go out regardless of the weather but it doesn't matter to them. They seem to enjoy getting muddy.

> Certainly the boys seem to go out more often than the girls but after all rugby is all about rolling about in the mud.

> I think it's a bit different for most boys. They seem to not mind going out in the cold. Probably boys are so much more active that they don't feel it the same.

Clearly these views do not reflect the reality of the situation as it would seem likely that many boys find cold, wet, muddy conditions as unpleasant as do girls. What emerged from the interviews with teachers, however, was the strength of the images and ideas held concerning the differences between girls and boys in relation to bad weather. Furthermore these images and ideas have definite implications for the teaching of girls physical education. For example in Heyfield School it was noticeable that *all* of the teaching during the observation period took place indoors, apart from the mixed soccer sessions, which were attended by a few fifth-year girls. In contrast the male department in the same school taught outdoor games regularly each week and the boys went on cross-country runs. The underlying assumption was that girls would be 'put off' by cold weather and, therefore, it was more successful to encourage them to be active in a warm environment. While this might have been a rational position it was based on gender-specific assumptions and *in practice* resulted in a far more restricted timetable than the *official* timetable of activities suggested. On many occasions the indoor alternative was relay races or the equivalent with two classes put together in one indoor space.

Showers

This aspect of physical education was considered because it is an issue which consistently produces negative responses from girls and has been identified as important in other research (Measor 1984). Shower facilities after physical education classes were available, in theory, for all schools. Ten schools included compulsory showers in their physical education teaching for first to fourth years with one school enforcing compulsory showers until the end of the fifth year. Therefore over two-thirds of the schools in the research did not have compulsory showers for any age group. Many commented that this was a change that had occurred over the previous ten years. Restricted time, inadequate facilities and the view that showering can create unnecessary worry and tension for girls were the reasons given for non-showering. As one head of department commented:

> By the second year showering becomes embarrassing because they are so self-conscious and embarrassed. I wouldn't make staff force kids through showers. I think it is one way to put girls off PE.

This is one crucial aspect of the relationship of physical education to young women's developing sexuality. However, the main justification for the removal of showers was a concern to save teaching time rather than any positive consideration of the embarrassment or humiliation caused to young women.

Aims and objectives

The heads of department were consistent in their stated aims for physical education. They offered three possible 'main aims': enjoyment, preparation for leisure and 'standards'. Thirty-one respondents replied that enjoyment and preparation for leisure were the two most important aims. These were seen to be closely interconnected: the following comments were typical.

> We aim to give them an interest in sport in general, something they'll enjoy doing so that they'll want to carry on in something when they leave school.

> I'd like to think that when they'd left they had found one activity that they enjoyed enough to keep up. My first aim is the enjoyment of the lesson.

To get them to enjoy physical activity so that they will continue it. Because if you enjoy something you will carry on. It is going to be good for you, healthy for you whereas if you do something you hate, you won't continue.

I'd say that participation and enjoyment are the most important aims of PE so that they will continue some activity throughout life.

In relation to 'standards' the main comments were as follows.

I can see for some people it is a good way for disciplining. Team games give good discipline.

I have very high standards and they are an important aspect of my teaching; punctuality, dress, appearance etc. I aim to encourage the girls to also have high personal standards.

PE aims to give social guidance. That's what we can do in PE – please and thank you, opening doors for people. Self-discipline is one of my main aims.

I think in PE rather than in any other subject it's teaching them manners, self-discipline, good appearance. I think we do a good job for the school more than any other subject. We're more disciplined than any other part of the school.

At Heyfield School the head of department stressed the importance of self-discipline, 'standards' and education for leisure. She put little stress on physical skill acquisition:

Self-discipline is one of the main [aims] and I think that is the hardest to get here . . . we have a whole week on manners – the kids need mothering, they need social guidance. That's what we do in PE – please and thank you, opening doors for people. These come before I even worry about what goes on in the gym or the sports hall. The children are not disciplined; they have no self-discipline . . . in ball skills for example they're not learning to throw the ball, they're learning to do what miss tells them when she tells them.

Further she recognized that this emphasis on manners and behaviour was not quite so strong in the boys' department:

The boys are not quite so pedantic over discipline as we tend to be. They spend more time playing the games.

As discussed above, a substantial amount of time was spent on enforcing and maintaining 'standards'. If this was a major aim, as claimed, then the fact that as much as half the teaching time was spent in its pursuit could be justified. Each lesson was prefaced by attention to kit, removal of make-up and jewellery, an insistence on silence and an orderly line before entering the gym or sports hall. On three occasions during the observation period no teaching at all took place due to problems in enforcing silence and the correct appearance. Significantly, the imposition of discipline consisted of enforced activity. On all three occasions the following week's lesson was replaced by a circuit of physical training and exercise in the gym. On one occasion the deputy head (male) was brought in to discipline the group first and then to observe their 'punishment'. It was revealing that physical activity was used as a punishment within physical education. This reinforced the observation that physical education consisted of very little physical exertion. In fact the only times that girls experienced any substantial physical exertion and showed symptoms of quickening of heart-rate was during 'punishment periods'. Yet many of the girls appeared to enjoy these circuits and were happy to leave the gym physically tired. Verbal admonition from the deputy head, given to a group following their 'misbehaviour', contained continual references to behaviour 'befitting young ladies'. The implication was that there was an acceptable form of behaviour and presentation directly related to their development as young women. In disciplining a second-year group he stated:--

> I am disappointed in you all. You should care about how you look – remember to bring your kit. You should take pleasure in your appearance, look and behave like young ladies! You are a disgrace to yourselves and the school.

At Rosehill School the observed practice also confirmed the stated primary aim of self-discipline and manners. Throughout the observation there was an emphasis on 'standing properly' in silence. It was clear that 'standing properly' related to the 'correct' posture associated with girls and their development as 'young ladies'. On two occasions when girls were lined up to leave the gym the staff commented:

> Walk out and leave the gym like Miss World. That's right, shoulders back, tummies in, show how good you look.

The aim of 'educating for leisure' was emphasized in the policy statements in all the observed schools although in practice the application of this aim varied in different situations. For example at Rosehill School this aim was realized partly through access to swimming as a major activity. Swimming was a popular activity in the options for the fifth and sixth forms and was an activity clearly transferred into their leisure time. However, the diminution of interest in physical education by the sixth form suggested that the girls and young women at this age were not enthusiastic to participate in physical activity as a leisure pursuit during school hours. They had the opportunity to select from a number of activities but only a few took part in trampolining and swimming.

The girls and young women were presented with no real direction towards possible opportunities in leisure. There were no posters specifically informing the girls about activities locally which could be of interest. They were directed to a local swimming club but this was a competitive option and was not available as an appropriate post-school leisure experience. Previously girls had been introduced to ice-skating and horse-riding (both 'female' defined sports) in the fourth and fifth years. However, this was dropped as

it was a lot of bother for staff so we keep them in school now.

The fifth-year options were offered as particularly 'suitable' or 'appropriate' for girls and their future interests. These were badminton, keep fit, trampolining and swimming.

At Heyfield School the head of department confirmed that a link between girls' physical education and their future leisure pursuits was desirable:

Social pressures determine it. Every book you open – *Woman, Woman's Own* – what diet are you on? What exercise are you doing? It's more and more now – there's the Pineapple Studios. More are doing it now – girls play squash and badminton. It's a social change – we've labelled keep fit 'aerobics'. We do aerobics and they think it's great. All it is is keep fit. They think it great 'cos Jane Fonda does aerobics and we do aerobics. We have to fit in to social pressures.

Physical education is viewed as fitting into social conventions and geared to maintaining the status quo.

In practice the activities offered to the girls in the fourth and fifth year *did* relate to their future leisure opportunities. The majority opted for badminton or keep fit/aerobics with a small group doing 'health and beauty'. Badminton and keep fit are high on the list of physical activities undertaken by woman post-school (Deem 1986) and 'health and beauty' is central to the culture of femininity. However, it is important to question whether physical education is or should be reinforcing or reproducing stereotypical women's leisure or should be challenging existing definitions of leisure. The research suggests that in the majority of situations physical education prepares girls and young women for gender-specific leisure pursuits.

At Townley School, single-sex and in a working-class area, the situation was slightly different. The physical education centre displayed many sport and physical activity posters and gave information on sports, how to get started, sports centres, local teams, and so on. The excellent facilities provided a wide range of activities both in curricular and extra-curricular time. There were traditional female physical education core activities plus canoeing, swimming, judo, archery, trampolining, badminton and volleyball. As the head of department stated:

> We offer as many activities as possible so that they might find something which they will have the confidence to continue after school.

In addition, a nearby sports centre was used for fourth and fifth years thus introducing the girls to a leisure complex and giving awareness of and familiarity with a community leisure setting.

However, even though the available activities reflected a concern with appropriate post-school opportunities, the majority of heads of department across the research authority, including Townley, identified a 'drop out' or diminution in interest of young women at 14 and 15.

> Up to the third year they're really keen. It's probably adolescence, more aware of lads, fed up of doing the same thing day in and day out. They just get turned off PE.

> There's a definite drop of interest in the fourth year but there again girls drop out of everything in the fourth year. The only way to retain interest is through a broad curriculum.

> Yes – girls lose interest in the third or fourth year. It's the social

idea of women and sport. Boys tend to continue to enjoy football, etc. but it's not the same for girls.

I know it's the classic one but it's the third year – past the Christmas term. They lose interest because they're doing things that they can't easily carry over. You get girls coming up to you and saying: 'What's the sense in us learning to play hockey – we'll never do it. What's the use in learning to run the 100 m: I'm not going to be a 100 m runner.' I suppose they just don't see the point. We also get complaints about the style of PE kit.

Clearly any interpretation of stated aims within physical education must accept the significance of gender and assumed roles. Important here is the relevance of organized physical activity in the lives of young and adult women. Does a loss or lack of interest in participation reflect a 'natural' biological predisposition? Alternatively, is the social construction of gender-specific behaviour particularly influential in affecting the interest of adolescent young women? While the relationship between the stated policies and the observed practices in the research schools are discussed in the next chapter, this section on aims and objectives raises several important issues in relation to gender and girls' physical education. These can be summarized as follows.

1 *The physical* – the development of physical skill was not considered by teachers to be of primary importance and this was confirmed by observation. The relationship of physical education to ideologies of the physical and male–female power relations emerges as a crucial area for analysis and discussion.

2 *'Preparation for leisure'* and *'enjoyment'* – the importance of these aims for contemporary physical education needs to be considered in relation to existing feminist literature and research on 'women and leisure' (for example Deem 1986; Wimbush and Talbot 1988; Green et al. 1990). Issues concerning the relevance of physical education to the experiences of adolescent girls and the influence of the social construction of sport or physical activity as a 'male' pursuit demand further consideration.

3 *'Standards'* – the importance of 'standards' (discipline, appearance, behaviour) in both the traditions and contemporary practice of girls' physical education raises important questions concerning the reproduction of ideologies of femininity and female sexuality.

Activities

Curricular activities

In relation to the activities taught in the five years of compulsory secondary schooling the most obvious feature to emerge was the existence in the first to third years of a common core curriculum across the majority of schools. This included gymnastics, netball, rounders, athletics, swimming, tennis and hockey. Dance was taught in twelve schools only in the first and third years and in fourteen schools during the second year. Team games continued to dominate the main programme of activities with netball and/or hockey, rounders and tennis played in the majority of schools in the first to third years. However, gymnastics remained the 'back-bone' of physical education with all but one school offering it throughout the three years. 'Gymnastics' can cover a-wide range of activities but when questioned all described the gymnastics taught in the lower half of the school as 'modern educational gymnastics'. However, several heads of department reiterated the adviser's comment that since the late 1970s gymnastics has become more structured than the educational gymnastics of the early 1970s. Swimming was taught in twenty-eight of the thirty-two schools in the first year but it was replaced in some schools in the second year and remained on the timetable of only fifteen schools by the third year. This reflected the lack of access to swimming pools for many schools and the economic restraints which have resulted in swimming being prioritized in upper juniors and the first year of secondary schools only.

During the fourth year a number of schools retained a commitment to the core activities which had formed the structure of physical education in the lower school. However, gymnastics lost favour in a large number of schools leaving it as an activity in only nine schools. Athletics was totally absent from the fourth year curriculum but netball (twenty-one schools), tennis (twenty-one schools), rounders (fourteen schools) and hockey (nine schools), all remained an integral part of the programme. The major change in the programme was the introduction of a wide range of 'leisure' activities (e.g. trampolining, volleyball, judo, keep fit, etc.). In twenty-one of the thirty-two schools the fourth-year activities formed a programme of 'options' in which the element of choice was introduced for the first time. This innovation since the early

1970s has been a direct intervention in order to provide a more interesting and relevant curriculum for adolescent girls and in response to the raising of the school leaving age (ROSLA) in 1972. The physical education teachers viewed this curricular change as being the most significant development in physical education in the 1970s and 1980s.

> Options have certainly been a positive development. Once you've introduced an option scheme, if it works successfully and if the curriculum is designed around the option scheme at the top end you can bring in lots of new ideas fairly easily whereas without the option scheme or you haven't got the staff available you stick to things that will keep the most occupied for the best length of time – which tends to be the traditional method.

> At the fourth or fifth year they need to know what they can enjoy and carry on. It is important that they aren't forced to go out and play hockey and they hate it. I'd rather they played table tennis, as long as they enjoy it. In lots of schools kids are forced – choice is a good thing. They must be able to make their choice.

> Options have come into the fifth year in this school where they are even discussing the fact that they might possibly come into the fourth year... Things like badminton and squash are becoming more important because more children play them outside of school.

By the fifth year the 'traditional' activities had become less popular with tennis and netball retained in fourteen and ten schools respectively but with swimming (six schools), rounders (three schools), hockey (two schools) and gymnastics (two schools) very much minor activities across the city. Overall the traditional team games for girls (netball, rounders and hockey) showed a marked decline in popularity after the third year whereas volleyball was played in eighteen schools in the fourth and fifth year in comparison to none in the first and second year and only one in the third year. Basketball remained a marginal activity with few schools (four in the fourth year and five in the fifth year) offering it to girls even in the upper school. This was primarily because netball was viewed by most physical education staff as the 'female' sport and basketball as the more 'suitable' male option.

> Boys don't want to play netball: they play basketball. That's a much more vigorous, spunky game. It's much more suitable for boys than girls.

> I do think there are definite boys' activities and girls' activities. Boys do basketball and we do netball, which I think is more suitable. The two are similar but I just think netball is more appropriate.

Not all staff necessarily saw netball as more physically appropriate but they did recognize the importance of tradition.

> I wouldn't think netball necessarily more appropriate. I'd say it's tradition because really in netball the first thing you are teaching them to do is stop. If we started with basketball it would be more relevant 'cos at least they could keep moving with the ball. Then there is more skill involved. However, netball is more traditional so that's what we stick with.

Tennis as a racquet sport formed part of the core curriculum in the majority of schools in the first to third years, was dropped by some schools in the fourth and fifth years, although it remained in fourteen schools in the fifth year. Thus more schools retained tennis in the fifth year than any of the other core activities, which reflected the recreational nature of the game. Certainly tennis, in both private clubs and public parks, is more accessible to many young women post-school than are other activities included in the core curriculum. Thus it was retained in twenty-two schools in the fourth year and in fourteen schools in the fifth year as an 'option' leisure-linked activity. Badminton, in contrast, was absent from any school in the first two years and then showed a dramatic increase, with twenty-nine schools including it by the fifth year. Once more this reflects the recreational aspect of badminton in that it is viewed as an activity that can be continued after school yet is not considered suitable for a physical education curriculum in the early years of secondary schooling. This can be linked to a general lack of indoor facilities which made it difficult for most schools to involve a large number of girls in badminton at any one time. Also it was considered by the staff as particularly suitable for adolescent girls:

> Girls like badminton when they're 14 or 15 because you don't have to use any energy or run around. It's just a case of putting the shuttle across a net.

> They're keen on badminton 'cos it's an easy option. They're indoors, warm, dry and they don't have to get hot and sweaty. It suits young ladies!

> I think badminton's popular because it fits in with their expectations

at that particular time. They can play at their own pace, they don't
have to concentrate – it's relatively easy.

This last comment from one head of department raises the interesting relationship between physical education and young women's
sub-cultures during adolescence. Certainly there appears to be an
explanation from many of the staff that young adolescent women
will not want to be active, get hot, work at a high skill level or
concentrate! The area of options and the change from lower school
to upper school, in relation to physical education, young women's
sub-cultures and teaching staff expectations, are important issues
concerning gender and physical education.

The research showed that whereas gymnastics and dance were
part of the core curriculum of the early years of secondary schooling for most girls, popmobility/keep fit/aerobics replaced them in
the fourth and fifth years. These latter activities have been brack-
eted together as there are no clear definitions in this area. In some
schools activities defined as keep fit were identical to another
school's popmobility programme. Popmobility, keep fit and
aerobics are recreational pursuits popular for their emphasis on
health and their suitability for young women. These activities are
very much 'feminine' pursuits almost exclusive to women. It is
interesting that no school offered the girls any 'masculine' equivalent – fitness training, circuit training or weight training. Keep fit
and aerobics were justified by many staff as a self-evidently suitable activity for young women.

> Keep fit is very popular now because they are very figure conscious.
> We use this to encourage the girls.
>
> Yes, girls want to do keep fit and aerobics at this time because they
> are conscious of their appearance and want to work at looking
> good.
>
> We can get the girls to do keep fit because it's the in-thing isn't it?
> They can get the fancy leotards and jogging suits. They see it as a
> means to improve their shape and make them look good.

Once again the issues of girls' developing sexuality is highlighted.
The emphasis on figure, appearance and generally 'looking good'
must be considered in relation to the literature on young women's
sexuality (Jackson 1982; Lees 1986). Radical feminist theory
(see Chapter 1) analyses the relationship of sexuality to women's

subordination in society. A critical examination of the teaching of girls' physical education must consider the theoretical implications of this for the practice of physical education teaching.

The period of observation in the case study schools confirmed the presence of a common-core curriculum in the first to third years and a system of options in the fourth and fifth years. On the whole, it was noted across all the schools that the lessons appeared to be enjoyed by the majority of the girls especially in the first three years. This was confirmed at Townley School where there was an overwhelmingly positive response from the girls.

It's great – the best lesson in the school.

I like rounders especially. It's a real good laugh.

PE's pretty good really. You know where you stand here and what to expect. You can't get away with anything mind or they'll have you.

The PE department is the best. They're strict but you know what you can do and can't do.

I like the teachers: they treat you okay.

Even within this positive atmosphere a range of issues relating to gender were noted. Three out of four staff continually referred to the girls as 'young ladies'. They were often asked to 'walk in like young ladies', 'imagine you're in a beauty parade'. Although there were positive reinforcements for female sport in the posters on display it was noted that examples of good practice were constantly given with male players or activities. For example, on four occasions male tennis stars were used as illustrations.

Notice how Borg stands when he serves.

Do you think you're McEnroe? – don't hit the ball so hard.

At no time were female tennis players used as positive examples. On other occasions the girls were encouraged to

Move your feet like a boxer.

Attack the net. Move forward with determination. It's like going for a goal in football – be positive.

However, it is interesting to comment on the judo sessions that were observed. These were taught by a judo coach rather than by a full-time physical education teacher. During the period of observation she took a small group of third years (approximately eight girls) as her usual fourth and fifth years were doing examinations. One class observed was a group of eight girls randomly selected from the bottom band of the third year. The girls were unenthusiastic at first but by the end of the session they were excited and keen to continue with the activity. The coach had a quiet manner and treated the girls with considerable respect and encouragement. She never shouted or raised her voice but was firm in her approach. She considered that, on the whole, girls were more successful to teach than boys as they 'used skill but not brute strength'. She had won all of her personal judo competitions against men up to black belt standard. Her style of positive encouragement and belief in the girls' abilities gained a positive response from the girls. They worked hard, soon left their 'giggly stage' and appeared to gain confidence and skill from the sessions.

The teaching style used in the judo sessions suggested that girls at this stage of adolescence responded well to positive encouragement and to a belief that they were capable of achieving high standards. Most interesting was the fact that when the girls were not subjected to gender stereotyping they gained confidence and a real acceptance of their abilities beyond the gender stereotypes of femininity. This indicates clearly that when gender stereotypes are challenged less gendered outcomes can be achieved.

Extra-curricular activities

Throughout the local authority extra-curricular activities were an extension of curricular time and the same activities were offered both at lunch time and after school. The general pattern was to organize netball, hockey, rounders, athletics and tennis teams, where these were taught in the formal programme, plus a gym club and a dance club. Schools that had a swimming pool on site offered a variety of swimming activities (e.g. swimming teams, personal survival awards and life-saving). One school offered a sub-aqua club. The main 'option' activity on offer in extra-curricular time was badminton (twenty-six schools), with a volleyball club organized in just four schools.

Heads of departments identified the main constraints on extra-curricular activities as lack of staff and facilities. As discussed earlier, the staffing problem was a particular concern to the female staff. Lack of commitment to girls' activities by women staff (other than the physical education specialists) resulted in fewer opportunities for girls to participate, a lower profile afforded to girls' activities and increased pressure on the female physical education staff in terms of time and commitment to a wide range of physical pursuits. Women teachers need to be 'Janes-of-all-trades' to ensure that a variety of activities are offered.

Traditionally inter-school team practices and matches have formed the backbone of the extra-curricular programme. John Kane (1974), in his national survey for the Schools' Council, found that of the teachers (male and female) involved in extra-curricular activities, 98 per cent were regularly involved in competitive team games. The research interviews with the heads of girls' physical education suggest that the organization and coaching of teams remain a priority in many schools. However, the research showed a change in emphasis away from inter-school competition. Nineteen of the thirty-two schools played far fewer matches than they did five years earlier. This was not due necessarily to teacher choice. All recognized that financial cut-backs and constraints were adversely affecting their programme of inter-school fixtures. More crucial, however, were the restrictions experienced by girls from a number of sources. Several heads of department suggested that there had been a steady increase in girls taking part-time evening and Saturday jobs. In particular, Saturday morning fixtures had decreased dramatically during the 1980s. Only six schools participated in a full Saturday fixture programme and consequently these schools were compelled to travel beyond the city boundaries to find opposition. One head of department commented:

> I never have difficulties getting teams out but I think that it is the type of girls we've got. It's nothing to do with me, it's just the type of girl. They don't have to have Saturday jobs and they are so keen and willing to take part. They have parental support and are proud to come and represent the school on a Saturday.

The inclusion of Saturday fixtures was related directly to the class location of the school. The schools which continued this tradition were the ex-grammar schools in the middle-class suburbs of the city or Anglican non-selective schools, also ex-grammar schools, drawing from the diocese. The growing divide between middle-class schools, whose parents' associations support and provide financial assistance, and schools which rely on local education authority grants, was made obvious by the provision of minibuses, team kit, tracksuits, etc., provided by organized fund-raising and parental contributions. Although all schools took part in some inter-school competition, primarily after school hours, a significant number of teachers noted further constraints on the participation of girls:

> A lot of girls are expected to do babysitting and get paid for babysitting and so it is an incentive for them not to come to practice and things. That's why we now use all the lunchtimes.

> When it gets dark we have to finish earlier. This applies to girls not boys. We also rarely have Saturday matches now, due to Saturday jobs.

> We have the problem of girls having to pick up younger kids and do the housework etc.

> There is a problem of away matches because parents don't like them travelling across the city in winter.

These constraints (domestic responsibilities, child-care responsibilities, protection of girls on dark evenings) influenced the participation of girls in the *full* range of extra-curricular activities, not just team games.

The research shows that although there may be some differences in staffing, organization and facilities, there are consistencies across the schools in relation to content, aims, objectives and the emphases brought out during physical education teaching. Many are related directly to *gender* and as the research progressed it became apparent that girls' physical education is a significant element in the process of the reinforcement and reproduction of gender ideologies through schooling. The following issues emerged as of particular significance.

First, mixed versus single-sex physical education – throughout the research, both in the interviews across the city and in the case study schools, mixed versus single-sex organization continually surfaced as significant in relation to gender and girls' physical education.

Second, the reinforcement of ideologies of the physical – physicality and sexuality – through the teaching of physical education. This issue is significant both in the historical material and in the contemporary research into stated policies and observed practices. It relates not only to *what* is taught but also to *how* it is taught and the emphases within physical education. In each research school, the core activities were the female-defined activities which had developed from the historical origins of the subject. However, it was the enforcement of gender-related 'standards' which was emphasized across *all* of the schools, irrespective of whether they were single-sex or co-educational, middle-class or working-class schools. These 'standards' were in terms of expected female behaviour and appearance and were reinforced through aims, objectives, policies and practices.

Third, the relationship of physical education to girls' leisure activities outside the school, the 'culture of femininity' and girls' future leisure opportunities. These issues are considered in more detail in Chapter 5.

Priorities, Policies and Practice: Major Issues in Physical Education

Co-educational physical education: the implications for girls

The teachers interviewed were unanimous in their concern about mixed-sex groupings but were not united in their desire to promote co-educational physical education. Indeed, the research evidence suggests that moves towards co-education remain primarily within the upper section of secondary schooling with a core single-sex curriculum taught in the first to third years. This is in contrast to the Inner London Education Authority study (ILEA 1984) into physical education which identified 'a general enthusiasm' for mixed teaching throughout the authority. The study was based on eight secondary schools teaching all or most of their curriculum in the first three years to mixed groups and twenty-eight schools organizing the fourth year upwards on a mixed basis (ILEA 1984).

The contrast between the research LEA and the former ILEA confirms that there are no consistent national developments in mixed physical education teaching. Such initiatives remain on an ad hoc basis. Apart from the ILEA initiatives, most developments have been dependent either on the enthusiasm and innovation of individual staff or on administrative convenience, particularly in the top years of secondary schooling.

As the research shows physical education developed historically as a discipline on quite distinctive gender lines with different aims and objectives. Until the 1970s physical education reflected a popular culture within which women's and men's sports and leisure activities were clearly demarcated and distinct ideologies of masculinity and femininity were continually reinforced. The mixed-sex initiatives in physical education which developed in the late 1970s and early 1980s have their foundations both in co-education or equal opportunities philosophy and in economic necessity. Since the 1960s within education in general there has been a trend away from the traditional single-sex secondary school towards co-educational comprehensivization. Although co-education was seen as important for ensuring equal opportunities for girls and boys across the school curriculum, physical education has remained predominantly single-sex in secondary schools and has received little critical consideration. Only in the 1980s, with the growing literature on various aspects of gender relations and schooling, has the issue of mixed physical education been on the agenda. The recognition that physical education is the last bastion of single-sex teaching in many co-educational comprehensive schools has encouraged researchers such as Rosen (1987) to comment:

> The case for mixed PE hardly needs to be stated . . . The guiding principle in schools should be that pupils must never be segregated by sex (or race, colour or any other innate character) unless there are absolutely compelling reasons for doing so. (Rosen 1987: 152)

Thus mixed physical education has been proclaimed as a progressive move towards the fulfilment of a complete equal opportunities policy in schooling offering equal access across all areas of the curriculum. As the research interviews with departmental heads indicated, however, a positive response to mixed physical education is by no means universal. There are indications that much of the mixed teaching in the research LEA, which took place primarily in the upper school options programme, was developed as much through economic necessity and the rationalization of limited teaching resources and facilities, than because of a committed educational philosophy.

The ad hoc basis of new initiatives was confirmed further by the lack of commitment to mixed physical education from within the LEA. Significantly in 1984, while the education authority was about to institute co-educational community schools throughout the city, the question of mixed physical education was ignored by those implementing the change. In answer to a question as to whether there was concern about it remaining as the only single-sex

subject on the curriculum within an authority openly committed to
co-educational teaching, one county councillor involved in the
appointment of new departmental heads for the reorganized authority replied:

> The Labour Party generally hasn't given any serious thought to that
> issue – not at all. If you've got these kids of 13 or 14 stripping off
> together – you can't have young bodies in that situation! It is really
> going to be at that level.

This statement suggests that when dealing with the 'physical', attitudes around sexuality rather than the politics of sexuality, over-
shadow education priorities and justifications. Clearly, it is not only
biological justifications for physical differences between boys and
girls, but also issues concerning sexuality which uniquely place
physical education in the debates over co-education and equal
opportunities.

The response within the research LEA is typical of the general
lack of thought and consideration given to physical education
in the broader co-educational structure. The concern and unease
expressed by the teachers interviewed over the possibilities of
reorganization into mixed physical education grouping centred on
several issues. First, they identified clear differences between the
teaching of girls' and boys' physical education. Commenting on
these differences, the adviser focussed on the differences between
women's and men's perceptions of physical education:

> I feel passionately that women's perception of physical education is at
> least as relevant as men's. We have quite different emphases – not
> just the activities we teach but also the ethos.

This view was reiterated by the majority of departmental heads. Further, the periods of observation confirmed that girls' physical education remains totally separated from boys, not only spatially but also
in perceived philosophy. Although the study had no formal contact
with male departments, women teachers argued strongly that their
departments were involved in separate and distinct areas of work.

John Evans et al. (1985) utilize the concept of subject sub-culture
developed by Stephen Ball (1987) in order to understand the differences between female and male physical education. This position
recognizes two distinct sub-cultures within the one subject area with
male and female teachers having 'quite different conceptions of how

and what to teach' (Evans et al. 1985: 6). The concern, shown by the women teachers in the research, was that implementing organizational change would not result necessarily in unified teaching. The gender-specific sub-cultures of physical education teachers would

> tamper only with the surface of educational practice leaving paradigmatic and pedagogic views and practice largely untouched.
> (Evans et al. 1985: 6)

Although developments in teacher training throughout the 1980s have resulted in a gradual change from single-sex specialist secondary physical education teacher training to mixed-sex courses, there is little evidence that a new ethos has developed within physical education which unites the two areas. Further, the women teachers interviewed had worked in the research LEA on average for eight years, the majority having trained in single-sex establishments. This demonstrates that even if new initiatives were emerging in teacher education, and this is an extremely doubtful assumption, it would take a long time for them to filter into the schools. In-service work is vital if major innovations are to take place in current school practice. Yet local in-service work can be influenced by the adviser and, as the interview evidence demonstrates, the advisers are a product of a traditional system committed to the ethos of physical education as it has developed from its historical roots. Thus physical education exists in a gender-differentiated form, ideologically and structurally underpinned by gender assumptions. The teachers are aware that the superficial merging of two separate identities will not result easily in the production of a new unified whole. Given the historical analysis and the contemporary interview material, which identifies the continuing strength of gender ideology at the foundations of teaching girls' physical education, their doubts and concerns are justified.

The second concern of the women teachers, with regard to mixed physical education teaching, was that the girls would reject such an innovation and its implications. The following quotes were typical.

> I am sure the girls themselves would not want to do it.

> The girls wouldn't be happy about it. They are terribly lacking in confidence and when the boys are around they're worse.

> It could be mixed but our girls have enough of the boys in class – our girls are quite happy to be on their own. How many times do you hear the girls ask to play with the boys? Never! They'll play out together at

lunch and after school quite happily but girls don't want to be with
the boys.

It's the middle years really when they don't [mix] and want to be on
their own with their own peer group. Girls don't want mixed games.
They'd also be too embarrassed.

These comments raise a number of significant questions. The main
reasons for believing that girls would reject mixed physical education relate to girls' embarrassment during adolescence and to their
lack of self-confidence. Although these are teachers' perceptions
rather than the girls' responses, the evidence from qualitative
research into mixed-sex teaching situations in other secondary subjects supports this concern (Spender 1982; Stanworth 1983; Mahony
1985). Madelaine Arnot (1984) succinctly summarizes the findings
of this range of research:

We get glimpses of the extent of boys' disruption of the classroom:
their noisiness, their sexual harassment of girls, their demands for
attention and their need of disciplining and their attitudes to girls as
the silent or the 'faceless' bunch. (Arnot 1984: 31)

The problem of sexual harassment (verbal, emotional and physical) is potentially intensified when dealing with activities which
centre on the physical. There is growing evidence that girls have to
cope with severe sexual harassment throughout their daily lives,
especially in mixed settings in schools. Although there were few
mixed teaching situations observed in the case study schools, many
of the teachers confirmed that girls and young women faced many
problems in mixed physical education. The annual mixed swimming
galas and athletics meetings were identified as a main focus of
harassment.

Oh, the girls have to put up with remarks from the lads. That's why
they all wear tee-shirts over their costumes while they wait for their
race.

You can see the boys eyeing up the girls and comparing them. The
girls are obviously aware of this – some of them just refuse to swim in
the galas. I think at a certain age they just prefer to opt out.

In these situations girls run the gauntlet of persistent comment on
their physical appearance and sexuality. While some girls respond
by attempting to hide their bodies by dressing in loose clothing,
many others opt out to avoid being the target of innuendo and sexist

comment. Clearly the assumptions about women's bodies, as objects to be looked at, admired and criticized, are intensified in settings of mixed activity, particularly during the sensitive years of adolescence.

This does not deny that boys face problems during adolescence with regard to sexuality, but while boys are judged by 'achievement' with regard to masculinity, girls are judged 'against' masculinity. Simone de Beauvoir's (1974) notion of 'woman as other' is clearly articulated in this instance with girls' physicality 'judged' against the boys. Given societal and cultural expectations of 'attractive femininity' – Connell (1987) refers to 'emphasized femininity' – girls are expected to respond to the stereotype in order to achieve male gratification. Their femininity is, literally, 'up for grabs'. There is a possibility that given sensitive, aware teaching, mixed physical education may provide a positive challenge to sexism in schools. However, its potential must be placed in context. This research has shown that the past and present structure and organization of teacher education, the practices of teaching in schools and the cultural demands on schools to reinforce the traditions of female–male behaviour, prevents mixed physical education from contributing to a less sexist experience for girls. On the contrary, it can condemn adolescent girls to an intensification of sexual abuse. Consequently the answer for many girls has been to opt out of physical education altogether. Further, the lack of self-confidence of girls' and the restriction on girls' participation in mixed settings is significant, given the evidence of research into classroom interaction. The indication is that boys have far more contact with the teacher, receive more attention, talk more in class and are much more 'visible' (Spender 1982). The evidence suggests that mixed physical education is not that different. Mixed grouping generates problems concerning levels of participation and degrees of confidence. In principle there might be equal participation but in practice girls are usually less involved. Observation of mixed lessons showed this to be the case. In both mixed volleyball and basketball classes the boys dominated the action with the girls only involved occasionally as active participants. Boys regularly control mixed settings:

> Generally we found that girls were tolerated by boys in the lesson as long as their contribution was kept within certain bounds and the boys didn't lose control . . . Another issue in ball game situations is the girls' involvement in the game. Many complained that the boys

wouldn't pass the ball to them in basketball and soccer. The boys freely admitted this to be the case. (Graydon et al. 1985: 3)

As has been noted in classroom-based work, the boys tend to make the decisions, are loud and demand more of the teacher's attention. Furthermore, as the teachers interviewed recognized, by the time children arrive at secondary school physical skills have been considerably influenced by their socialization and junior teaching. Many of the teachers noted that on average girls at 11 do not start from an equal position to boys either in terms of physical skill or hand–eye co-ordination. In many cases girls have not been encouraged to develop ball skills and have been taught literally to 'throw like a girl' (Young 1980). This does not mean that girls are incapable of reaching similar skill levels but that mixed teaching, given the available evidence, seems unlikely to assist with this development. The teachers recognized many of the potential problems of moving towards co-educational physical education in schools. The adviser raised further important issues:

> One of my big worries is that there are already more men teaching PE than women for the 11–15 year olds. The problem I can see is that if it goes mixed then there will be fewer women teaching, especially with the fact that a woman's career structure is often interrupted. I can see men moving in if we aren't careful.

These serious reservations concerning women's jobs and status are justifiable. Statistics on the position of women teachers on pay, status and promotion point to considerable inequalities. This is marked particularly with regard to the percentage of women in senior management positions as head teachers, deputy heads and heads of departments in comprehensive schools. In schools where there are separate departments, the evidence shows that in the majority of cases the male is overall head of department (Evans and Williams 1988). In the research LEA the tradition of separate girls' and boys' physical education (reinforced by the fact that it is one of the few authorities with male and female advisers) resulted in a woman head of department for girls' physical education in all the schools. However, in 66 per cent of the co-educational schools studied, the male head of boys' physical education was on a higher salary scale than the girls' head of department. While women teachers held status within the girls' department, in the majority of schools the male head of department had higher status and ultimately power concerning physical education within the context of the whole school. Given the evidence from co-education in other subjects, the concern about the career prospects of women staff, and their potential loss of control over girls' physical education in a move towards mixed grouping within one joint department, is justified.

Further, loss of control by women teachers in mixed settings has been exacerbated by economic constraints and cuts in education. John Evans and Trevor Williams (1988) suggest that women teachers are more likely to leave their jobs or take a career break. Over one-third of the women heads of department in the research study had taken a break from teaching for childbirth or family responsibilities. If this trend continues in those departments teaching the same activities to girls and boys, there is a danger that women will be replaced by men. Evans and Williams (1988) also found that the ideology of 'familism', the view that the family is where women should experience their self-fulfilment, remains pre-eminent in views about and responses to women physical education teachers who are mothers. This ideology generates substantial constraints on women's career opportunities. This research demonstrates that such ideology is not solely a male construct. For example, the female physical education adviser stated:

> After all women have far greater family commitments than men. Women used to take time out to have a family but now they stay with maternity leave. Maternity leave is the biggest load of rubbish. I know it might be old fashioned but I think no household should have both parents in full-time jobs.

Given the recent consolidation of ideologies of motherhood and domesticity and the substantial structural constraints on women in contemporary British society, any move towards mixed physical education must be treated with caution, particularly with respect to the status and career opportunities of women teachers. Observation of mixed physical education together with an awareness of alternative research in this area suggests that organizational innovation towards co-education teaching must be critically assessed. Equality of access through organizational policy does not automatically result in equality in outcome and practice. Mixed physical education does not necessarily create a less gendered *structure* of girls' physical education nor *experience* for the young women on the receiving end. Girls' physical education must be considered within broader feminist theoretical analyses of schooling and women's position in society.

Ideologies of physicality and the politics of sexuality

This research was initiated as an attempt to extend recent research on the relationship between schooling and the maintenance of a sexually differentiated system of power relations (e.g. Deem 1980; Spender 1982; Stanworth 1983), to include a consideration of physical education. Throughout the research two interrelated constructs have been central to the analysis: physicality and sexuality.

Physicality

Although physical education may have contributed historically to the liberation of girls and young women in relation to dress, opportunities for physical activity and access to a future women's profession, physical education also reaffirmed clear physical sex differences in ability and capacity within generalized boundaries and limitations of women's sexuality. In 1979 an HMI report confirmed that

> PE is the part of the curriculum that can contribute to the *physical experience of the pupils*. Its aims are concerned with the development of psycho-motor competence in order to facilitate participation in worthwhile activities during the critical years of puberty and maturation to adulthood. Its unique contribution is that it focuses on the body and on experience in activities in which bodily movement plays a significant part. (Flanagan 1985, emphasis added)

In this statement no distinction is made between girls' and boys' physical education. Yet there is a need to unpack what the 'physical experience' means for girls in physical education.

The research confirms the continuing dominance of stereotypical assumptions about girls' and women's physical abilities. As was shown in the interviews with women teachers, girls are frequently portrayed as weaker and less powerful than boys, while the desirability of feminine grace, poise, finesse and flexibility is stressed. Also it is clear that physical activities which were developed historically to encourage such feminine virtues (e.g. dance,

gymnastics, netball) continue to dominate the core physical education curriculum. Neither the stated policies and priorities nor the
observed practices stressed the development of psycho-motor com-
petence as suggested by the HMI report. Indeed the period of
observation in all four case study schools reinforced the notion that
girls are not stretched physically either in skill acquisition or, more
specifically, in the development of physical strength and general
fitness. Indeed, in Heyfield School physical effort was used as a
punishment for misbehaviour rather than as a positive and necessary part of physical education (see Chapter 4). This finding confirms recent evidence which reports growing professional concern
about the lack of physical fitness and skill development of children
in schools and questions the standards and motives of contemporary physical education.

Yet the issues of health, fitness and skill acquisition *are* pertinent
especially for girls and young women. While ideologies of the physical remain embedded in the policies, priorities and practices of
physical education, a construct of 'female physicality' is produced
and reproduced. This has implications not only for a critical examination of future physical education teaching but also for an understanding of male–female physical power relations as an integral and
crucial aspect of patriarchy.

Physical power relations

Until recently feminist theory has concentrated on male–female
power relations without including or defining a politics of physical
power. Cynthia Cockburn (1981) suggests

> Socialist feminist theory has abandoned a concept of the superior
> physical effectivity of men on account of a very reasonable fear of
> that biologism and essentialism which may nullify our struggle. I
> suspect, however, that we have thrown out something we need with
> the radical feminist bathwater. We cannot do without a politics of
> physical power. (Cockburn 1981: 4)

Explanations for physical sex differences based on biological
determinants have been the subject of much academic, as well as
popular, debate (Ferris 1978; Dyer 1982). Whether differences in
physical ability primarily are biologically determined or socially
conditioned remains controversial albeit, to some extent, irrelevant.

What has become increasingly clear, and this was emphasized by the physical education teachers in the research, is that physiological differences between girls and boys, women and men, are seen as 'natural' and 'inevitable' rather than socially constructed and culturally reproduced. Furthermore, differences between women or between men are not considered to be as important as those identified across the sexes.

Ideas about physicality, however, are not restricted solely to common-sense assumptions, 'achieved' by some individuals and challenged by others. Taken collectively they form ideologies of the physical which are formulated and articulated in cultures of masculinity and femininity. For the experiences and regulation of women it is the institutionalization of an ideology of the physical – incorporating ideas about their biology, physiology and psychology – which comes to define 'womanhood'. In the criminal justice system, media, health service and *schooling* this process is powerful in constructing, reinforcing and maintaining gender divisions in society. Further, this ideology of physicality is central in restricting and subordinating women in all aspects of their participation in social practices. Such restrictions are experienced by women at a range of levels. First, through a virtual monopoly over physical strength and technical capacity men maintain control over technology and manual occupation. Cynthia Cockburn (1981) suggests:

> The appropriation of muscle, capability, tools and machinery by men is an important source of women's subordination, indeed it is part of the process by which females are constituted as women. (Cockburn 1981: 14)

In a more thorough and developed account of her research into the male domain of the printing industry she argues:

> Small biological differences are turned into bigger physical differences which themselves are turned into gambits of social, political and ideological powerplay . . . women are first tendered weak; the weakness is transformed to vulnerability; and vulnerability opens up the way to intimidation and exploitation. It is difficult to exaggerate the scale and longevity of the oppression that has resulted. (Cockburn 1983: 204)

This emphasizes the social construction of female physicality and the consequent cycle of oppression. Further, ideologies of the physical reinforce women's dependency in domestic situations. The image of the male 'handyman' (i.e. changing the tyre, mending the fuse and performing physically 'skilful' tasks) remains prevalent. In reality women perform many arduous domestic tasks but these are defined as 'everyday' mundane chores. The sexual division in the home, and the ideology which supports it, leaves women dependent on men to perform the more 'skilful' or 'craft'-based jobs.

However, ideologies of the physical have consequences at a more threatening and direct level concerning men 's physical control and domination of women. Physical violence by men is a threat for all women and a reality for many. Many women are restricted by and fearful of rape, assault and harassment. Consequently the restriction on the social freedom of most women is pronounced. This physical advantage over and oppression of women is maintained at an ideological level. The strength of ideologies of the physical makes many situations of male sexual harassment and violence appear inevitable. Men's physical power is an acceptable feature of male sexuality:

> Women's experience of sexual and/or physical intimidation and violence – much of it the result of what is assumed to be typical male behaviour – is an integral part of women's lives.
>   The physical and/or sexual abuse of women is a manifestation of male domination itself, it has been seen to be a natural right of man. (Stanko 1985: 70)

The importance of contemporary feminist research on male violence is that it identifies *physical* power relations at both *ideological* and *political* levels and places sexuality as central to the analysis and understanding of women's oppression. Male physical dominance is identified as an integral part of male sexuality used directly or indirectly to control and discipline women.

Sexuality

Female and male sexuality each incorporate an ideology of the physical which has become internalized and a generally accepted part of everyday life, appearing to be both natural and inevitable. Male sexuality can have a multi-dimensional control over the social lives of women.

> By defining us in terms of the space we may move in, by dictating the way we look, by restricting the work we do and how and when we do it . . . and by constraining the social life we engage in. The effect is to

undermine our confidence and reinforce our inferior status, to alien-
ate us from our bodies and to induce a timid and careful response to
men. (Coveney et al. 1984: 19)

The ideology of the physical which is specific to female sexuality is
constructed around assumptions about strength and appearance. In
terms of the generally accepted stereotype of 'ideal female sexuality',
women are expected to be passive, dependent and vulnerable yet
remain responsible for their own sexuality. As Ros Coward
comments:

> It is acknowledged that women have a sexuality but it is a sexuality
> which pervades their bodies almost in spite of themselves. It is up to
> women to protect themselves by only allowing this sexual message to
> be transmitted in contexts where it will be received responsibly, that
> is, in heterosexual, potentially permanent situations. (Coward
> 1984: 2)

Further, in their appearance women are defined in terms of sexual
attractiveness. For women the primary objective in relation to the
'physical' is to look good for others and, most significantly, for men.

> Every minute region of the body is now exposed to this scrutiny by
> the ideal. Mouth, hair, eyes, eyelashes, nails, fingers, hands, skin,
> teeth, lips, cheeks, shoulders, arms, legs, feet – all these and many
> more have become areas requiring work. Each area requires potions,
> moisturizers, conditioners, night creams, creams to cover up blem-
> ishes. Moisturizer, display, clean off, rejuvenate – we could well be
> at it all day, preparing the face to meet the faces that we meet.
> (Coward 1984: 81)

Female sexuality stresses the need to be attractive but not physically
or sexually active. Women who project their sexuality through dress
or style and promote active sexuality are unacceptable and 'dangerous'. They are 'looking for trouble'. Ultimately it is women who are
responsible for morality. The harassment of prostitutes and the
stigma and debates around prostitution highlight this polarity
between 'normal' and 'dangerous' women. In discussing the case of
Peter Sutcliffe (the so-called Yorkshire Ripper), Lucy Bland (1984)
notes:

> With Jayne's death came press and police horror that the Ripper had
> made an 'error' in his killing of an 'innocent', perfectly 'respectable'

victim. By implication, prostitutes were deemed non-innocent, non-respectable victims, who had brought death upon themselves. (Bland 1984: 187)

Female sexuality, incorporating expectations around appearance and behaviour, is an integral part of the traditions and contemporary policies and practices of girls' physical education. In each school the case study observations noted an emphasis on 'standards' of appearance, presentation and specific 'ladylike' behaviour. For girls and young women, physical education reinforces one primary objective of the 'physical'; to look good for others with a central concern for personal appearance. Although physical education is not concerned directly with the time-consuming quest for the 'ideal' feminine appearance as described previously by Ros Coward (1984) there remains a central emphasis on 'acceptable' feminine standards of appearance and presentation of self. The introduction of an option course in physical education entitled 'health and beauty' in one of the case study schools represented an attempt to maintain adolescent girls' interest through an emphasis on the culture of femininity. Clearly in this situation, the definition of 'physical' education is taken to include an emphasis on appearance and 'beauty'.

The message in relation to female sexuality remains clearly articulated through physical education. Women's bodies are physically developed in order to look good and presentable, particularly to men. Yet they must be protected from over-development and physical contact in order to avoid 'unnatural' or 'unhealthy' touch and danger to 'delicate parts'. Attempts to impose this ideological construction of the 'ideal woman' are clear in physical education practice. As the case study observations showed, a considerable amount of the total teaching time is devoted to discipline over appearance and to ensuring correct dress or uniform.

For a long time young women's anxieties concerning physical education have centred on embarrassment caused by showering after a lesson. When asked to reminisce about their former physical education experiences, it is common for women to comment on their negative memories of showers. Explanations for the problems faced by young women in coping with showering and 'exposure' are clearly grounded in physiology and the physical changes of puberty. However, it is the interaction of physical development and cultural expectations which is important. It is not the actual physical changes

of the young women's bodies which cause the anxiety but the culturally determined responses to these changes. Those who are 'in-
between' or average in their development can cope with their
situation. They meet the expectations for desired shape and
development. Those who deviate from the expected norm face acute
embarrassment and, often, unkind comment. Given that there is a
societal emphasis on the desired physique for adult femininity, those
who became aware of their differences during adolescence are
caused anxiety and often retreat or 'hide' from public scrutiny. Traditionally, physical education has provided the context in which
physical differences have been unmasked and made public. Most
adult women are not expected to expose their bodies and are encouraged to dislike their body shape unless it conforms to the 'ideal'
feminine stereotype. It is interesting that the research indicates that
showering no longer remains a central aspect of the physical
education lesson. The removal of showers is justified for institutional and organizational reasons rather than as a positive move to
avoid embarrassment or humiliation for the girls. Yet it is a sad
cultural reflection that girls and women should be uneasy with their
own and other women's bodies. In terms of health and hygiene,
showers *should* be a part of physical education. However, the 'problem' for physical education involves confronting a culture of femininity which creates embarrassment and concern while attempting
to encourage positive attitudes to hygiene and girls' perceptions of
their own body image.

This situation is made more complex due to a situation highlighted at Townley School. Here it was parental pressure which
stopped showering. Parents were concerned not only that girls
would be forced into being naked in a group situation but, most
importantly, that physical education staff would be able to watch
their daughters in the showers. This reaction implies not only a
concern to protect their daughters' sexuality (i.e. a protected,
hidden heterosexuality), but also a homophobic assumption that
female physical education teachers' heterosexuality is 'questionable'. Clearly the stereotype of the lesbian female physical education
teacher is linked to the 'masculine' definition of physical activity
or sport (Lenskyj 1986). Women who undertake physical activity,
develop strength and muscle and have chosen a career in this area
are stereotyped as having 'questionable sexuality'. This implies
lesbianism and its assumed non-feminine attributes. Sue Lees (1986)

found similar situations in her research on adolescent girls and cites many instances of girls taunted with 'lezzie' chants.

Clearly ideologies of the physical and the politics of sexuality create problems for physical education, the result of which is that physical education reinforces its links with 'acceptable' femininity and sexuality in order to challenge the stereotype of physical education as 'butch', 'masculine' and, inevitably, lesbian. Physical education upholds an 'ideal' sexual image of women defined as

> not of a demure, classically 'feminine' girl but a vigorous immature adolescent. Nevertheless, it is not a shape which suggests power or force. The sexually immature body of the current ideal . . . presents a body which is sexual – it 'exudes' sexuality in its vigorous and vibrant and firm good health – but it is not the body of a woman who has an adult and powerful control over that sexuality. The image is of a highly sexualized female whose sexuality is still one of response to the active sexuality of a man. (Coward 1984: 41)

Physical education, more than other subjects on the curriculum, encourages girls to be 'vigorous', 'vibrant' and to develop 'good health' but often within the constraints of an ideology of the physical which sets limitations on female activity and physical contact and concentrates attention on personal appearance. Together this contributes to the development of acceptable female heterosexuality. However, it must be stressed that this is by no means straightforward or simplistic and there is no inevitable determined result from this process. Many teachers and pupils experience conflict through working in an area centred on 'the physical', with the potential to develop a positive female physicality, yet with the limitations of powerful social and ideological expectations relating to cultures of femininity. There are resistances and negotiations, thus demonstrating that it is not a totally determined or inevitable process.

In the mid-1970s, as the 'second wave' of feminism became established, Simone de Beauvoir (1974) defined the objectification of the female body and its subsequent inactivity:

> The ideal of feminine beauty is variable, but certain demands remain constant, for one thing, since woman is destined to be possessed, her body must present the inert and passive qualities of an object. Virile beauty lies in the fitness of the body for action in strength, agility, flexibility, it is the manifestation of transcendence animating a flesh

that must never sink back on itself . . . Her body is not perceived as the radiation of a subjective personality, but as a thing, sunk deeply in its own immanence; it is not for such a body to have reference to the rest of the world, it must not be the promise of things other than itself: it must end the desire it arouses. (de Beauvoir 1974: 178)

Today 'fitness of the body for action in strength, agility, flexibility' remains the ideology of male physicality. Men's control over women is generated by an acceptable heterosexuality reinforced and justified by this ideology. For women the ideology of the physical is, as Simone de Beauvoir suggests, constrained in action and experienced as subordinate to and, especially in appearance, defined by men. For women to develop the basis for achieving equality they need to gain control over their sexuality. Implicitly, this requires a redefinition of the 'physical' for both men and women. Physical education can and does contribute to this dominant definition of woman-as-object. Not only must physical education critically relate its teaching to a feminist analysis of physical power relations but also it must use this analysis to instigate positive change for girls and young women. The physical is central to patriarchal power relations and women's subordination, and thus physical education within schooling is in a unique position to challenge the structural relations and social arrangements of oppression and inequality.

Young women's sub-cultures: leisure and physical education

'Loss of interest': biological v cultural explanations

As discussed in Chapter 4, 'loss of interest' in physical education was confirmed by the majority of heads of department interviewed in the research. The following statements reflect this concern.

girls at this stage are going through . . . they're changing fairly rapidly. They get embarrassed very easily. They change shape more and feel more self-conscious than lads do. They just lose all interest in physical activity at this time, it's just natural.

Once in the third or fourth year many girls just don't like physical activity much. They'll do it but only because they have to. They're more interested in other things – boys, discos, I suppose.

I've talked to my girls and they always say 'we're just beginning to be interested in outside'. They lose interest in PE at school. If they go to a disco they expend more energy than they ever would in a PE lesson.

The most common explanation for 'loss of interest' was that it is 'natural' – an inevitable, developmental problem inherent in adolescent young women. The stereotypical view of young women during adolescence is that of significantly less commitment to physical activity than young men, a period of development characterized by lethargy and inactivity. The research indicates that this stereotype is a gender expectation which cuts across class and ethnic divisions (although articulated to different degrees) and physical education teachers tend to generalize the stereotype and apply it to all young women. While this may reflect the reality of the experience for many girls, the explanation must involve more than a simplistic biological determinism. It is clear that young women experience certain biological changes during puberty, a process which occurs on average between the ages of 9 and 13. These developments are dramatic, often including major changes in body shape and they are related to the onset of menstruation and occur over a relatively short period of time. The findings in the case study schools emphasize this point with regular comments by teachers on the differing physiques of girls in the first and second year classes. How far these biological changes influence young women's responses to physical education is debatable. For example, it is now widely accepted that in most situations menstruation does not directly affect women's ability to participate in physical activity.

What is more important is the social construction of women's biology, the ideology of biology (i.e. the expectations placed on young women as to how they should be reacting to these changes). It is reasonable to assume that for some young women the changes of puberty produce such distinct changes in body shape that it becomes difficult to retain the levels of mobility and movement which they developed as children. Again, this is confirmed in the research from the observations carried out in the gymnastics lessons. However, it is important to emphasize that social and ideological pressures, linked to sexuality and body physique (as discussed earlier in this chapter), together produce inhibitions on mobility and movement rather than biologically determined restrictions. Young women's developing awareness and exposure to the culture of femininity reinforces an expectation of the 'physical' defined by inactivity, passivity and neatness. This culture of femininity is accepted by the majority of physical education staff and it is intensified by peer group pressure. The small friendship group, identified as crucial to the reinforcement and maintenance of the culture of femininity (McRobbie 1978; Griffin 1985), influences the take-up of activities in physical education. While a young woman may retain an interest in playing netball or swimming in the team, it is often pressure from friends which encourages her to 'drop out' or, at best, diminishes her enthusiasm. On several occasions in Heyfield and Townley Schools it was evident that girls did not attend extra-curricular activities for these reasons:

> No one else will do canoeing so I'm not.
>
> They've not got their kit.

Certainly many potential senior team members are lost, not through lack of personal interest or commitment but because of the sub-cultural influences and pressures experienced by young women.

Teachers' responses

In theory many teachers explain the conflict and loss of interest by girls in biological terms. In practice they tackle the issue by reiterating their belief and commitment to the values and ideals of the physical education on offer. Participation is enforced primarily through compulsion and discipline. This was apparent in all the schools observed, although the need to discipline and enforce standards varied according to the class location of the school. Archway School was particularly 'successful' in maintaining participation through firm discipline. However, it is impossible to determine through observation whether participation can be equated with continued interest and motivation. Although the majority of the girls at Archway took part in the physical education lessons without too much resistance, it remains significant that as soon as compulsion was removed in the sixth form the numbers of young women continuing with physical education dropped dramatically. It is questionable whether interest and enjoyment, placed so high by all physical education teachers on their list of aims and objectives, can be achieved by use of hierarchical or disciplinarian methods.

A second strategy adopted by teachers to alleviate any conflict between physical education and young women's experiences was the adaptation of the curriculum to make it more 'relevant' to the needs and requirements of young women. Options for older girls were used in this way. In all the schools within the authority the bulk of the 'options' comprised of individually based activities which were recognized by the teachers as being 'more appropriate for older girls'. The observation period emphasized that option sessions were primarily indoor activities, justified as 'an activity which won't mess up their hair or make them too sweaty'. Indeed, observation in all the schools suggested that the majority of physical education for girls was becoming indoor based, primarily to avoid disaffecting girls and to reduce any potential conflict. The above quote typifies the response from teachers in that care has to be taken not to challenge too seriously the culture of femininity and its emphasis on appearance. The ideology of female physicality sets clear guidelines which relate to appearance and behaviour which must not be transcended. In some schools the activities introduced into the curriculum related directly and purposefully to appearance and to the development of an 'attractive' figure and body shape. Keep fit was offered as an upper school option in most of the LEA's schools and an extreme example of an 'appropriate option' was the introduction of the 'health and beauty' course in Heyfield.

The main issue raised by these developments is that they are derived from, and directly reinforce the cultural expectations of femininity. Once more as McRobbie (1978: 52) suggests, young women become 'both saved by and locked in the culture of femininity'. The message that is being transmitted in these situations is that young women should not be interested and involved in physical activity in order to develop strength, muscle and fitness, rather they should be concerned with enhancing their appearance (i.e. in making themselves more 'attractive' to men). Consequently teachers, in order to negotiate the potential conflicts between physical activity or physical education and the culture of femininity, create situations which avoid confrontation while reinforcing the cultural definitions of femininity which prevail elsewhere in the school and outside in the wider community. Teachers are trapped within this difficult dichotomy.

Girls' and young women's resistances

Many girls and young women adopt gender-based resistances to schooling centred on their appearance or a 'silent, sullen stare' (Griffin 1981). In physical education, resistances based on appearance develop intensified forms. Young women who use their appearance to challenge their school experiences confront physical education by contesting its central ideological tenet. In each of the schools researched there were occasions when young women refused to wear the required uniform. They wore make-up and jewellery and refused to obey the 'golden rule of physical education' (i.e. tying long hair back). These challenges to authority were more obvious in the changing room than elsewhere in the school. Potentially they produce confrontations specific to the physical education situation. While other teachers can choose to ignore the wearing of a ring or earrings which contravene school regulations, physical education teachers not only uphold their own standards and values concerning appearance but also have the added concern (which can involve litigation) for safety during physical activity. Rings, earrings, necklaces, badges and long hair are dangerous in a range of physical activity; injury potentially carries the professional, and possibly civil law, charge of negligence.

The 'sullen stare' described by Griffin (1981) is of particular significance in physical education. A sullen, silent 'participant' on the netball court or in the gymnasium, effectively 'opting out' of the activity, is inordinately difficult to manage. In the classroom a young woman using the 'sullen stare' often simply encourages dismissiveness or indifference by the teacher. In mixed groups, where boys tend to dominate the lesson and receive more attention from the teacher (Spender 1982; Standworth 1983), a silent, female member of the group provides little overt challenge to the success of the lesson. Indeed it reinforces the view of the stereotypical female pupil as being passive, quiet, less articulate and disinterested. In physical education, however, where some degree of lively, active behaviour is demanded, a silent, sullen participant produces far more conflict and this affects the participation of the group. It was observed to be a particularly successful form of resistance by adolescent young women, in that it caused considerable disruption.

Towards a feminist explanation for the relationship of
physical education to young women's sub-cultures

What becomes increasingly clear in relating the theoretical analysis of young women's sub-cultures to the priorities, policies and practices of physical education in secondary schools is that biological explanations for young women's loss of interest and resistances, as given by many physical education teachers, are inadequate. While acknowledging the physiological changes of puberty, an understanding of cultural expectations is vital to an understanding of young women's experiences, attitudes and behaviours. It could be argued that the physical education on offer to young women is, to some extent, in conflict with their interests and attitudes not simply because they are undergoing biological changes of puberty but also because the cultural expectations of gender-specific attitudes, behaviour and role are at odds with both what is on offer and the values, ideals and ethos which underpins the subject.

The research shows that physical education continues to be dominated by team games. Team games are seen as synonymous with sport which is problematic for female participants. The relationship of sport to masculinity is well documented (Young 1980; Hargreaves 1982). Sport celebrates a specific expression of masculinity, with its sporting heroes dominating the headlines on the sports pages of all newspapers. For young women a culture of femininity and romance is reproduced and reinforced through the magazines they read, the television they watch and their everyday experiences. Physical education appears incompatible with their expected lifestyle and the expectations of 'young womanhood' in popular culture. Sport is portrayed primarily as a male pursuit and participation in sport remains locked into masculine values. Young women spectate, support and admire; they do not expect, normally, to participate. Furthermore, team games are problematic for young women not only by definition but also in form. Young women's cultures which emphasize the 'best friend' or small groupings do not relate easily to team situations, particularly as teams tend to be selected for them, whereas they are free to choose their own friends. Physical education stresses collective identity through team sports, gymnastic clubs, dance groups and athletic teams. Young women often reject these situations as being incompatible with their expectation of adult femininity. Young, fit, 'virile' men are expected to revel in group camaraderie and team spirit. It is less acceptable for adolescent women.

One of the primary aims of physical education was stated as 'preparation for leisure'. Yet defining leisure for women is also fraught with difficulties. Rosemary Deem (1984) questions the very existence of 'leisure' for women as it has been defined traditionally. Women's leisure is constrained by many factors and both the public and private spheres of women's experiences must be understood. The notion of 'preparation for leisure' is problematic for many women, especially in the realm of *physical* leisure activities. Rosemary Deem's (1984: 6) research confirms this, for in her study of 168 women drawn at random from the areas of a new town, she found 'scarcely any adult women who continued with any sport or physical activity done at school once they had left, with swimming the only widespread exception to this'. Similar statistical evidence can be found in *Social Trends* (DHSS 1985) and the Sheffield study of women's leisure conducted by Eileen Green, Sandra Hebron and Diana Woodward (1987). Therefore 'preparation for leisure' is a dubious objective for young women's physical education unless it is approached through a critical analysis.

The emphasis on leisure as a realistic objective for young women seems ironic given that many physical education teachers, as recorded in the interviews and confirmed in the case study schools, recognized their own personal limitations on time and opportunities in their private lives. Many of the teachers described the problems they faced concerning family and domestic responsibilities which restricted their opportunities to spend more time on extra-curricular activities or personal leisure pursuits. The failure to assess realistically the problems of using leisure as a relevant and useful concept for women produces a contradictory and, in many ways, an unachieveable aim for physical education. Teachers need to look more critically at both structural constraints and the realities of everyday experiences for women in physical leisure activities. The recognition by the teachers of a *gender* division of leisure as well as a sexual division of labour is an important issue for the teaching of girls in schools.

Finally it must be stressed that the crucial relationships between physical education, physicality and sexuality (discussed earlier in this chapter) are central to a feminist explanation of the relationship between physical education, leisure and young women's sub-cultures. The issues relating to showering, uniform and homo-phobia have to be considered if physical education is to relate to and understand the complex transition from girlhood to womanhood and the integral conflicts and confusions this creates for many young women. Physical education fails to provide 'meaningful experiences' for many young adolescent women because it appears at odds with the prevailing culture of femininity and does not realis-tically link with women's future leisure participation. It is accept-able for the girl labelled as 'tomboy' in junior school or lower secondary school to participate in and enjoy these activities but it is not acceptable for this ascribed status to persist in the transition to adult femininity. However, the common-sense perception of phy-sical education – as involved in the physical, concerned with the development of muscle, sweat, communal showers, childish asexual kit, low-status activities – in practice is not so simplistically repro-duced. Physical education is a subject which centres on physical activity which in our society is male defined and low-status for women but attempts to circumnavigate these crucial issues by reinforcing a culture of femininity which has been shown to be inherent in its traditions and continues to be reproduced in its con-temporary practice. As shown, therefore, physical education remains trapped within possibilities which may 'appeal' to young women but at the same time reinforce the culture of femininity.

CHAPTER 6

Conclusion: Future Policy, Future Directions

This book was conceived and initiated with the aim of examining and analysing the relationship between gender and girls' physical education. Clearly this relationship is significant for the experiences of girls and their eventual participation in sport and leisure activities as women. It is of particular importance given that physical education is the only separate and distinct curriculum area in secondary schooling which remains predominantly single-sex taught by women to groups of girls and young women. Also, it has inherited particular historical traditions which inform this unique separation. Unlike many other curriculum areas in which gender differentiation has been researched and analysed, girls' physical education is a subject area exclusively concerned with girls' experiences, which provides a curriculum for girls normally taught by women. One project cannot cover all aspects of schooling and there is work to be done which considers in depth the experiences and *responses* of girls and young women to physical education. Also, there is parallel work to be developed on boys and young men and the relationship between gender, sexuality and masculinity in the context of physical education.

Four significant dimensions of inquiry and analysis have developed out of my research project:

1 teachers' perceptions, attitudes and ideas
2 institutional analysis
3 the historical context of contemporary debate
4 cultural responses and resistances.

All four dimensions have proved crucial to the development both of a theoretical understanding of gender *and* an informed, critical analysis of the teaching of girls' physical education. Gender and girls' physical education are in a dialectical relationship in which gender is identified as a central construct of girls' physical education, the analysis of which provides an essential contribution to the theoretical debates concerning gender. The project emphasizes the importance of the connection between theory, practice and politics. For example, the research identifies the need to recognize and assess the importance of physical power relations as part of the social relations of gender. This has been considered both at a theoretical level and at the level of everyday practice in girls' physical education teaching. Arising from this consideration is the question of whether and/or how the social relations of gender could be challenged or modified through the transformation of girls' physical education. In other words, whether the politics of girls' physical education can include strategies and policies which not only will change girls' physical education but also will contribute to changes in the social relations of gender.

Theory, Practice and Politics

Teachers' perceptions, attitudes and ideas

The interviews identified the presence of powerful assumptions about femininity in relation to girls' and young women's physical ability/capacity, sexuality, motherhood and domesticity. These gender stereotypes were accepted and explained by most heads of department interviewed as being 'natural'. This 'naturalism' was defined as either a biological or a cultural inevitability. The interpretation of gender differences as 'natural' is surprising particularly with regard to physical ability/capacity, because the reality is so obviously different. The stereotype of girls as weaker, less powerful, neater and more precise in their movements is factually inaccurate. The research observations confirmed that the physical differences within one sex are far greater and more obvious than those between the sexes. Furthermore, the appearance of many of the teachers themselves was in direct contradiction to their own stereotyped views, as many were strong, powerful, muscularly developed women. Bob Connell (1987) argues that in understanding gender, 'nature' is often used as a justification rather than as an explanation. This suggests that the teachers felt the need to justify their practice of stereotyping and used biology as an explanation even though their own reality and experiences were at variance with their views. What this suggests is the existence of a powerful ideology of biology which will be considered in more detail later in this chapter.

A major explanation put forward for gender stereotyping is sex-role theory, which concentrates on the importance of socialization and sex-role learning. This is a central consideration within liberal feminist analysis. As discussed in Chapter 1, however, there are many critiques of this perspective emphasizing the lack of an adequate theorizing of power relations within liberal feminism; the neglect of an historical analysis; the over-reliance on individualism and voluntarism; the tendency to reduce gender to the biological dichotomy of male and female (Connell 1983; 1987). The research project contributes to an understanding of both the strengths and weaknesses of theoretical analyses which focus on socialization and sex-role stereotyping.

At a positive level, the research on teachers' perceptions is important in that it describes how teachers hold and promote expectations based on gender stereotypes. In considering attitudes and ideas the research confirms that women teachers have clear expectations about girls and young women which are constructed around a notion of 'femininity'. This 'femininity' encompasses ideas about physical ability/capacity, sexuality, domesticity and motherhood. Crucially the research demonstrates that it is a construction which does not remain simply in the minds of individual teachers but one which is generalized, both informing and influencing physical education practice. This is reflected in the choice of 'suitable' activities for girls, class organization and teacher – pupil interaction. Clearly then in their professional practice, women physical education teachers are agents of socialization, transmitting gendered messages to pupils through their interaction, language and teaching. It is a process derived from expectations around femininity.

It is necessary, however, to return to the criticism of this analysis. While research into attitudes and ideas contributes significantly to an understanding of the importance of gender in girls' physical education, at the level of description, it fails to give an adequate account of the *relationship* involved. In focusing on attitudes and ideas there is a tendency to concentrate on *differences* between the sexes. The teachers interviewed emphasized differences between girls and boys (both physical and social) and the importance of these differences in practice. Given their training this position is understandable, but if the analysis remains limited to this level, there is a danger of considering femininity and masculinity as polar opposites, thus assigning girls to ascribed roles and behaviour by using the dichotomy of sex as its organizing principle. The 'problem' of gender then becomes reduced to biological sex differences. What is missing here is the vital element of *structure* and, implicit with this, an understanding of power relations. Girls' physical education cannot be studied divorced from its historical and structural context. It does not exist in a vacuum influenced only by individuals with 'free-floating' ideas that can be changed simply by raising awareness and challenging attitudes. Such initiatives are significant but they need to be located and analysed within the broader relations of ideology and situated within contemporary structural and institutional contexts. The 'tip of the iceberg' has been illuminated by researching attitudes of teachers but the broader underlying structural complexities require further investigation and analysis.

Institutional analysis

The case study material, obtained from periods of observation in the selected schools, concentrated on the daily reality of teaching physical education in its institutional setting. From the evidence it is clear that gender is a significant factor in the structuring of girls' physical education, which can be identified through its organization, staffing, facilities, aims and objectives and curricular content.

However, the research also contributes to an understanding of the structures of gender as power relations. Three significant areas emerged from the research, each of which is concerned with the wider social relations of gender rather than solely with the specific context of gender and girls' physical education. Although, for ease and clarity of discussion these areas will be discussed separately, it is acknowledged that they are interrelated, overlap in many cases, and cannot be viewed independently.

1 Patriarchal power: the importance of the 'physical'
The research set out not only to identify gender differentiation but also to investigate the contribution of girls' physical education to the

reinforcement and maintenance of patriarchal power relations. Two important issues emerged which warrant consideration. First, it is necessary to question the use of 'male' power as a definition of structural power relations. There is a tendency, not surprisingly, to associate power with all *men*. While acknowledging that this is an accurate application in many, or indeed most situations, the power of men over women cannot be viewed as a universal and inevitable theory of domination. Hester Eisenstein (1984) introduces the concept of 'false universalism' to describe literature and analysis which talks of the experiences and subordination of all women regardless of other structural relations such as race, ethnicity, class and age. Similarly, 'false universalism' can be applied to the notion of 'male power'. Yet there remains a need for a concept that adequately describes the relevance and importance of patriarchal power relations without resorting to simple biological reductionism. The significance of this research project is that it identifies the presence of gender power relations in an area which usually is exclusive to women. In fact everyone concerned with the research – advisers, teachers and pupils – were women. Therefore it is not direct, overt 'male power' which is identified in the teaching of girls' physical education but, as Bob Connell (1987: 43) observes, the power of 'hegemonic masculinity' or 'the maintenance of practices that institutionalize men's dominance over women'. Interpreting hegemony is crucial to this analysis and is well defined by Raymond Williams (1977) drawing on the work of Gramsci:

> hegemony supposes the existence of something which is truly total, which is not merely secondary or superstructural, like the weak sense of ideology, but which is lived at such a depth, which saturates the society to such an extent, and which, as Gramsci put it, even constitutes the limits of consciousness for most people under its sway, that it corresponds to the reality of social experience. (Williams 1977: 27)

Gender needs to be theorized as being structured by a dominant hegemonic masculinity which not only forms the basis of male – female relationships but also is conveyed and internalized through institutions and social practice. Girls' physical education does not exist in isolation outside the hegemonic order. Despite being a female insitution, it remains an institutional form which internalizes, supports, maintains and reinforces hegemonic masculinity.

The second area identified by the research is the centrality of physical power relations as a construct of hegemonic masculinity. There is a clear relationship between men's physical activity, prowess, strength and contemporary western definitions of masculinity. This relationship finds particular expression in the competitive sporting world. Within feminist literature the importance of men's power has been defined primarily in terms of economic, social and political power. However, the research highlights the need to define a politics of *physical* power with the physical as a central construct.

The recognition that ideologies of the physical contribute to the definition of woman-as-object and reinforce women's physical subordination both at the overt level of physical violence and confrontation and at the more subtle level of self-confidence, bodily awareness and the stereotyping of women as weak and passive, should underpin all analyses of gender power relations. The relationship between girls' physical education and the structures of gender as power relations must be recognized both for future educational policy *and* feminist politics. Not only are physical power inequalities experienced as direct physical force and violence but also they contribute to that aspect of hegemonic masculinity which defines women as weak, passive, inactive and, inevitably, submissive. Women in authority (e.g. teachers and advisers) are part of that hegemonic process and, as the research shows, can be significant agents in the conveyance of gender ideology. By focusing on an aspect of social practice which is concerned with the body and physical activity, biological explanations for the totality of gender differences can be challenged effectively. As noted in the research, one of the reasons sport and physical education have been neglected by feminist analyses is that research that focuses on the body and physical action is assumed to be rather too close to biology for comfort! As Bob Connell (1987) points out:

> Even to speak of contradiction between social process and the body is not to have moved far enough from doctrines of natural difference and biological determination. For this is still to treat the body as unmoved mover, as what is fixed in relation to what is fluid, as what gives meaning and does not receive it. The body in relation to the social system seems like the monster looming outside the bright lights of the space station, alien and immovable, compelling by its sheer presence. (Connell 1987: 83)

The research, clearly related to 'women's bodies' and women's physicality, stresses the need to move away from analysis which focuses on assumed 'differences' and to recognize how social practice can be easily reduced to biology by emphasizing and naturalizing difference. The interviews demonstrate the strength of ideologies of biology which find expression in and are conveyed via the teaching of girls' physical education.

2 Sexuality

Throughout the research the significance of sexuality to an understanding of both gender and girls' physical education has appeared consistently important. What is apparent is that the construction of an 'ideal' heterosexuality is a crucial aspect of the structuring of gender relations. Physical education is a major influence in the process of sexualizing young women as heterosexual 'objects'. This finds expression in the persistent concentration on appearance, clothing, specific behaviour and desirable body shape which, taken together, contribute to the reinforcement of 'feminine' heterosexual appeal. 'Sexuality' for girls and young women does not develop in isolation; it is a social construction with male heterosexuality of central significance in its formation. As Bob Connell (1987) argues, 'emphasized femininity' is the response to the dominance of 'hegemonic masculinity'. Girls' physical education is shown by the research to be part of the social process whereby girls and young women, during the period of adolescence, are encouraged to develop an 'acceptable' feminine sexuality organized around heterosexual appeal, desire, objectivity and subordination. This is not a simplistic, over-determined process readily received and incorporated into the lives, experiences and behaviours of all young women. These structures and relations of gender power are by no means totally determining but are complex and also produce strategies of resistance and negotiation in girls and young women. It remains important, however, to identify the structural relations of gender within social institutions and practice. Girls' physical education contributes significantly to the maintenance and reinforcement of a subordinate 'feminine' sexuality and as a consequence feminist analyses of schooling should recognize girls' physical education as potentially a most significant site for the building and maintenance of gender and sexuality.

The research also shows that an analysis of gender must include

sexuality as a central concern. Adult femininity is intricately tied
to a constructed and compulsory heterosexuality. Again, research
which focuses on the body and physicality contributes significantly
to this understanding. The body and sexuality are not related simply
through biology but through the social construction and use of the
female body as a sexual object, be it an object of 'desire' or an object
of reproduction (O'Brien 1981). Adolescence is a vital period in the
lives of young women. Physical and biological changes have a pro-
found and social significance. At this stage of physical development
and sexual maturation women's bodies become public property,
developed for and controlled by others. In many spheres women's
bodies are on show, open to comment and abuse. The body moves
to public ownership and control which for many young women
creates private anguish. The conflict for young women at this stage
is immense. Unless they conform to 'ideal' femininity in relation to
appearance and presentation of self, they are open to verbal abuse
and their sexuality becomes questioned and scrutinized. Physical
education provides a situation where 'the body' is on show and
therefore at its most vulnerable. This is evident in the recognition by
women teachers that many young women have to face comment
and abuse in mixed settings such as swimming galas and athletic
meetings. However, this 'public possession' of, or public control
over, women's bodies is not a 'natural' development – a biological
inevitability. It is part of hegemonic masculinity whereby men can
gain and maintain control over women, not only in relation to their
sexuality, but also in relation to the use of social space. Physical
education in secondary schools must be made conscious of this
conflict for young women and recognize how it contributes to the
maintenance of hegemonic masculinity. It is not necessarily a conscious reinforcement but through the language used by teachers and
the organization of physical education (content, kit, changing
rooms, etc.) the conflict between body image and ideal femininity is
emphasized.

3 Division of labour

So far the structural analysis has focused on patriarchal power relations, physicality and sexuality. Throughout the research, however,
it became apparent that an analysis of gender and girls' physical
education should consider the relationship between schooling and
other social institutions. It is clear from the research that female

teachers and female pupils are influenced considerably by family relations. The sexual division of labour within families whereby women, as wives, mothers and daughters, bear the major responsibility for both domestic work and child-care, was identified as having major implications for teachers and pupils in physical education (e.g. opportunities to participate, extra-curricular programme, teacher career structures, and so on). Economic power relations, however, are not restricted to the family. They encompass all aspects of the sexual division of labour, existing in the workplace, in the community and at all levels within education. In girls' physical education, despite being a subject exclusively female in its teaching and practice, the relative financing of male and female departments is also significant. The research shows that where the female and male departments coexist in a mixed school, there is often gender differentiation both in terms of salary scales and status. Even though girls' physical education has its own history and cultural context, it is usually the male department which retains and wields the economic power. Where there are two distinct departments in a school, the holding of economic status and power by the male departments often has implications for the future development of the female department. The research highlights the need to consider carefully the staffing implications of initiatives such as mixed physical education where economic power and status are likely to move increasingly into the male physical education world.

Much of the literature on the relationship between schooling and the sexual division of labour concentrates on the place of schooling in the preparation of girls and boys for differential positions within the labour market. However, it is not only the transition from school to work which warrants attention. This research shows that there is a need to understand the *sexual division of leisure*, particularly in the transition from school to leisure where future opportunities and leisure experiences are concerned. The research shows girls' physical education contributes to a gendered leisure and sports experience for women. Clearly gender divisions in leisure are not solely dependent on girls' experiences at school but their physical education experiences are a significant part of their reproduction. It is interesting to note that for girls this is often a negative experience, whereas it tends to be positive for boys. In constituting a critical analysis of leisure, other institutional contexts are significant (i.e. family, sport, etc.) but it is clear that girls' physical education is central to the development of these complex and interrelated determinants.

Consideration of the 'division of labour' and the 'division of leisure' emphasizes the need to theorize the complex relationship between gender and class. Although the research is concerned primarily with gender and girls' physical education the class location of schools, teachers and pupils emerges as significant. Throughout the research the impact of class on the experiences of both women teachers and female pupils was evident. The inadequacy of analyses which concentrate solely on class, incorporating gender as a secondary determining structure, or which point to the universality of patriarchy and relegate class to the periphery, is confirmed in this research. Certainly hegemonic masculinity and sexuality have been discussed and shown to be important, regardless of class location. It is important to stress, however, that gender, through ideologies of femininity and the material of masculine power, is not static, pregiven and experienced as a common, universal form. While gender both constructs and is reinforced by girls' physical education it is constantly cross-cut by class location and it is dependent on specific contexts for its expression and influence. This conclusion is closest to feminist analyses which identify capitalism and patriarchy as comprehensive social systems which interact, and are most usefully defined as constituting a capitalist patriarchy (Eisenstein 1984). While this brings the theoretical understanding of the complex interaction of class and gender no nearer, it contributes research evidence to the proposition that an analysis focusing on an understanding of capitalist patriarchy provides the potential for a more adequate, coherent and comprehensive theory of social relations. Most importantly, this research contributes not only to the theoretical debates around gender but also to the politics of action. Although starting from an analysis of gender relations it is clear that a feminist analysis of girls' physical education, which is to inform and change practice and politics, must take into account the complexities of both gender and class.

While the research illuminates the need for an integrated analysis of gender and class, the neglect of race throughout the research has become apparent. Again, the research shows that the analysis of gender, within a schooling system which is a predominantly white, middle-class, male institution, must attempt to theorize the interconnections between gender, race and class. Black feminists (Hooks

1980; Carby 1982; Amos and Parmar 1984) have correctly identified the ethnocentrism of much feminist analysis and research. The research project began with a concern to explore the relationship of gender and girls' physical education but it concludes that race and institutionalized racism needs to be incorporated into future work in this area. Certainly the research shows how aspects of gender cut across race divisions and are experienced by all girls and young women. Throughout the research, however, there has developed a growing awareness that black Afro-Caribbean and Asian girls and young women need to have their experiences situated more centrally within analyses of gender and race relations and that structures of race and racism cannot simply be added to the analysis. One outcome of this research is the recommendation that there needs to be future work which considers the experiences of black young women particularly in relation to the teaching of girls' physical education.

The historical context of contemporary debate

In discussing sport in North America, Helen Lenskyj (1986) comments:

> Medical professionals played a major role in determining those sports and levels of participation that were safe for female anatomy and physiology. Not coincidentally, these activities were seen to enhance femininity, a socially constructed and historically specific concept encompassing personality, appearance and comportment. Acceptable activities promoted the physical and the psychological characteristics that males, as the appropriate dominant sex, pronounced appropriate and appealing for females: general and productive health, heterosexual attractiveness, passivity and conformity. *On all these issues, physical educators*, sports administrators, journalists and the general public *treated medical opinion as the voice of reason and authority*. (Lenskyj 1986: 139, emphases added)

Similar influences can be identified in the development of girls' physical education in nineteenth-century Britain. The roots and underpinnings of this female subject, as noted, are centred on male medical opinion which was conveyed and institutionalized as ideologies concerned with girls' physical ability/capacity, motherhood/domesticity and sexuality. It is important to situate contemporary analysis within its historical contexts in order to recognize that 'structure is not pre-given but historically composed' (Connell

1987: 63). Further it is important to realize the historicity of gender relations in order to challenge the 'false universality' of gender. An historical analysis contributes to a fuller understanding of gender and girls' physical education, because it demonstrates that 'femininity', while continually present and central, is not a fixed or an immutable category. The identification of gender in girls' physical education in the 1980s and 1990s cannot be interpreted as identical to that which emerges from historical accounts. Femininity is not to be equated with some transcendant biological category of being a woman but is both socially constructed and historically specific.

However, by identifying the influence of male professionals and the strengths of ideologies of gender on the development of girls' physical education, it becomes possible to understand the part played by this subject in the institutionalization of gender rather than understanding gender as simply the manifestation of attitudes and ideas held by unenlightened individuals. Girls' physical education is another aspect of schooling in which gender has become institutionalized and is conveyed through the practices of everyday teaching. Thus historical evidence gives weight to the argument that a structural analysis of gender and girls' physical education is crucial while identifying where change and negotiation can and does take place.

Cultural responses and resistances

Feminist structural analysis identifies how gender is determined and reproduced by the structures of patriarchy and/or capitalist social relations. However, this research suggests that this analysis is inadequate. Although gender can be shown to be reproduced through the institution of girls' physical education, structured by a hegemonic masculinity, this is not the whole story. The research also highlights aspects of girls' physical education which involve resistance and negotiation to the structures of gender. All girls do not accept passively the definitions of femininity which place them in a weaker and physically subordinate position. Teachers are not all passive agents within a process of cultural reproduction. In their responses and practices some women staff negotiate gender stereotypes and encourage girls to develop and challenge 'femininity'. Girls resist some of the institutionalized definitions and practices of girls' physical education which relate to femininity (appearance, suitable 'ladylike' behaviour, and so on). Although this research did not set out to investigate girls' responses to physical education the periods of observation in schools show that girls' physical education is by no means a straightforward process of gender ideology and identity reproduction. The research identifies the structures of 'patriarchal power', 'sexuality' and the 'division of labour' as central to an understanding of gender – girls' physical education being an institutional form which maintains and reinforces these structures. Also, however, it identifies the need for a cultural analysis which allows for those involved to resist, negotiate, and indeed, transform both the institution of physical education and ultimately the structures of gender. While the research identifies the power and influence of hegemonic masculinity over girls' physical education which maintains, reinforces and reproduces femininity, it also demonstrates the potential of resistance and challenge. It is with this potential that the foundation of transforming girls' physical education and the social relations of gender can be laid.

Future policy, future directions

Many strategies for increased participation and interest adopted in girls' physical education are based on their potential appeal to young women (e.g. health and beauty, keep fit). Inevitably such strategies reinforce the culture of femininity, locking girls' physical education within an 'emphasized femininity'. However, the research also shows that girls' physical education has the potential to develop policies and directions which could transform physical education and provide a platform for building resistance to the culture of femininity. The case studies highlighted the autonomy of physical education within the overall school system. Physical education departments are usually situated away from the rest of the school, the heads of department have authority over the curriculum and, in most instances, the teaching is carried out in a private sphere unfettered by the restrictions of examinations or the critical eyes of school hierarchies. Thus girls' physical education has the potential for change even within a schooling system which is becoming more rigidly defined by central government interventions and the National Curriculum. Gaby Weiner and Madelaine Arnot (1987) comment that

> Teachers have played a central role in challeng
> sexual divisions of schooling . . . . Teachers' p
> change and the long history of teacher inspired in
> referred to or acknowledged. (Weiner and Arnot

I would agree that it is possible for physical
initiate change although the stereotyping by, anu ...
tudes of, many women heads of department illustrates that change
will not be automatic or straightforward.

Two main approaches have emerged as challenges to sexism and
gender differentiation in schools: an equal opportunities approach,
concentrating on equality of access to all educational benefits (girl-
friendly); and an anti-sexist approach concentrating on girl-centred
education with its main objective being the relationship between
patriarchy, power and women's subordination (Weiner 1985). The
'equal opportunities' approach encompasses initiatives in girls'
physical education which emphasize equal access to facilities,
activities and curricular/extra-curricular time. Co-educational
grouping is one organizational change which is increasingly being
developed in order to ensure equality of access. As pointed out in the
discussion of mixed physical education initiatives, there are problems with strategies based on equal access which fail to question the
structures and power relations of the institution to which equal
access is sought. 'Equal opportunities' initiatives stem from a liberal
feminist perspective on gender and schooling. Gaby Weiner (1985)
articulates the main criticism of this approach:

> Expanding equal opportunities is not just a question of juggling
> resources or rearranging option choices . . . To liberalize access to an
> inadequate system may be acceptable in the short term but for more
> permanent change a major restructuring of all social institutions,
> including schools is needed. (Weiner 1985: 10)

However, it is important to acknowledge that some 'equal
opportunities' initiatives, introduced by teachers committed to
reform, represent an important political response to generations of
limitations imposed on young women in all aspects of school and
related activities.

Pessimism in the face of structural and institutional inequalities
provides no route towards change. Although this research firmly
establishes that a feminist analysis of gender and girls' physical
education must be situated within a structural analysis of capitalist

chy it acknowledges the usefulness of some short-term
tegic reforms. Indeed, unlike Gaby Weiner (1985), who draws
ear-cut boundaries between the inadequate equal opportunities
approach and the more long-term radical anti-sexist strategies, this
research recommends that strategic gains can be made in both areas.
The important issue is that policy does not remain locked into an
equal opportunities approach but must work towards a more radical restructuring of girls' physical education in order to attempt
to transform the power bases of gender identified throughout the
research. This challenge is not a straightforward task. The power-
less can attempt to appropriate their rightful situation but for the
powerful to relinquish their position demands considerable material
change. As Bob Connell (1987) recognizes:

> In a gender order where men are advantaged and women are disad-
> vantaged, major structural reform is, on the face of it, against men's
> interests. (Connell 1987: 285)

Further, although this research and its recommendations are concerned with gender and girls' physical education, a more integrated
strategy for change must also be recognized. Theoretically the
research is located within a framework which neither identifies gender as *the* dominant social relation nor as a secondary factor in
relation to primary class inequalities. The complexities of the interrelationship between gender, class and race are essential to the analysis, and changes in the structure of gender relations should be
concerned with structural inequalities of race and class. Consequently the connections between and across institutions and strategies for institutional change should be analysed and developed.

Progressive initiatives in girls' physical education must be made
with the awareness of the need for long-term fundamental changes
in the structures of the family, the labour process, sport, leisure, and
so on. At first sight this appears to be a substantial and unattainable
objective. The importance of inter-institutional links, however,
points towards more positive directions. There is considerable evidence to demonstrate that young and adult women's experience are
not totally determined by structural inequalities. Since the early
1970s there has been a substantial shift, through the development of
new directions, in the reconstruction of women's sexuality and
consciousness. These include the development of self-help groups
in medical care and mental health; the emergence of well-woman

clinics and other all-women projects geared to giving women more control over their own health and bodies. Women's groups have developed, resisting male violence through rape crisis centres, women's refuges and counselling. Within education new initiatives, such as 'new opportunity for women' courses, 'outreach' projects and women's writing groups, have emerged and have encouraged women to gain confidence and assertiveness in intellectual situations. The availability of self-defence and assertiveness training and women's fitness programmes, geared to developing health, strength and physical well-being, rather than the stereotypical construction of 'femininity' around appearance and body physique, gives women greater control over their physicality. These latter developments indicate a qualitative shift in definitions of the 'physical'. Women in these programmes are reclaiming the right to physical development and appearance on their own terms rather than on the terms laid down in the traditions of 'feminine culture', learned and reinforced in youth and, as this research shows, in their physical education experiences at school. Helen Lenskyj (1982), describing her own experiences, suggests that after years of upbringing women are

> alienated from our bodies not knowing the extent of our physical strength and endurance and not daring to find out. Those of us who have dared have found a new avenue for self-realisation as women and as feminists – joyful at the discovery that our bodies are strong and resilient, capable of hard work and hard play. (Lenskyj 1982: 6)

Advocates of girls' physical education should not rely on 'emphasized femininity' in order to encourage young women to participate. Not all young women are steeped in a deterministic feminine mentality and developments in adult women's projects should point the way towards more optimistic initiatives. The historical analysis shows that girls' physical education and women's sport in the nineteenth century contributed positively to a redefinition of women's femininity and, in particular, women's physical potential. While this remained within the clear boundaries of 'acceptable' behaviour, women's struggles in the twentieth century have shown that women can challenge inequalities at all levels. Girls' physical education has the real potential to challenge contemporary patriarchal definitions of women's submissiveness, passivity and dependence. While this is not straightforward the following recommendations provide a foundation for future policy directions. These recommendations are not ranked but should be interpreted as the basis for constructive moves to a more critical and radical feminist form of physical education teaching:

1 girl-centred organization
2 female-only space
3 collectivity and confidence
4 physicality: muscles, strength and physical power
5 consciousness-raising
6 future research.

These recommendations will now be discussed in more detail.

Girl-centred organization

The earlier discussion of co-educational grouping indicates that girl-centred organization should be retained. This raises the problem of retaining boy-centred organization in male physical education and its attendant implications. In the short term, however, girls require both the space and the time to develop their potential. In some instances this could involve the retention of a single-sex programme as the norm throughout the secondary school with selective periods of mixed teaching, if appropriate, for specific activities. It is crucial that the politics of gender and sexuality are understood by the staff involved in mixed activity sessions. With sensitive, understanding teaching, which may require positive intervention and leadership, mixed grouping can provide the forum for increased pupil aware-ness of gender issues and also can challenge existing gender expecta-tions and inequalities. If single-sex grouping remains the long-term goal, then the future is bleak for a comprehensive overthrow of gender inequalities. Yet there needs to be a short-term strategy to ensure girls receive opportunities, time, space and understanding to redress the traditional base of gender imbalance.

Female-only space

This is linked directly to the arguments made for girl-centred organization. For it is not only the formal organization of single-sex grouping which must be retained but also the provision of informal female-only space. Girls and young women need space to develop their confidence and realize their interests and to be in control of that social space. In co-educational schools the evidence shows that boys and men dominate space, physically and verbally, in all social situations (Young 1980; Spender 1982). In both co-educational and single-sex schools the main female-only space is in the toilets, the cloakrooms and the changing rooms. These are the areas where young women 'hang out', where they spend time together away from 'the lads' and/or the teachers. It would be a positive move for women physical education teachers to recognize the need for young women to have their own space for conversation, making plans or simply 'having a laugh'. Clearly this poses problems for school organization and the enforcement of school rules and regulations. However, as Townley School showed, it can be a positive move to open up changing rooms and facilities during breaks, lunchtime and after school, to provide open access to extra-curricular time and to encourage girls and young women to use the space available for their 'leisure' whether it be 'formally' for netball and table tennis or 'informally' for chatting with a friend. Too often young women's access to the physical education wing is restricted solely to participation in organized, formal activities. It would be a significant development to enable young women to develop greater control over their extra-curricular activities and therefore provide the space for meeting and socializing without interference from boys or teachers. A further symbolic – and practical – policy change would be to allow girls effective choice concerning clothes worn for physical education. The research shows that formal kit or uniform remains the norm. While there are arguments for and against school uniform it is clear that, within specific safety guidelines, adolescent girls should be able to determine appropriate clothes for physical activity. The earlier discussion argued that from puberty girls come to experience their bodies as 'public property' – defined, compared, criticized and often degraded. Within physical education especially, given the contexts of movement, girls need to have effective control over the 'presentation' of their physicality in dress and style. Consequently, teachers need to develop a greater sensitivity to and awareness of the pressures on young women regarding body shape and appearance. Young women's bodies are on display during physical activity and physical education teachers must realize the ease with which they can contribute to the alienation of young women with regard to their bodies.

Collectivity and confidence

The unifying feature of the women's projects mentioned previously is the emphasis on collective support. Physical education is in an ideal situation to offer young women opportunities for collective support through co-operative and enjoyable physical activity. While the relationship between teacher and student inevitably will reflect an institutionalized power relationship based on age and status, young women can be encouraged to work closely together, and with their teachers, through activities such as dance, outdoor pursuits and self-defence. Many boys and young men thrive on their collective 'rugby club' experiences. Indeed hegemonic masculinity is sustained and reinforced by male collective experiences. Young women also need the space for collective physical experience while rejecting and challenging the competitive 'macho' values of the male sporting ethos. This emphasizes the need for women to gain access to the positive aspects of the sporting world. These positive aspects include collectivity, co-operation and a sense of community, all of which can be encouraged through physical activity. Adolescence is a time to develop group and collective experiences rather than the channelling of young women into individually based activities which deny opportunities to develop group confidence and ability. This is particularly important for young women where group membership and experience tends to be played down. Physical education can contribute to developing a sense of solidarity between young women, thus defining a female-based construct of confidence and motivation. In many ways the 'movement' approach of girls' physical education prevalent in the 1960s and 1970s, and to some extent perpetuated in schools today, has emphasized these qualities. Where it has failed, however, is in its tendency to reinforce gender stereotypes and to emphasize gender divisions while encouraging a level of co-operation and a sense of community.

What is clear is that equal access to the contemporary sporting world would involve access to male-defined dominant, aggressive institutions. Physical education needs to take a lead in the encouragement of a redefinition of male-dominant sport. Clearly, such a proposition is idealist in its construction. Sport in British society is dominated by competition, commercialism, sponsorship and professionalism. Revolutionary change would be required even to begin to challenge a sporting world predominantly controlled and defined by men and situated within a capitalist economic structure. Yet change within sports institutions has to be a long-term objective for feminist struggle, given that sport directly reinforces and reproduces hegemonic masculinity. Part of this long-term struggle must come from physical education within the schools, at both primary and secondary levels. Changes in sport institutions will not come from policy introduced from the 'top' or dominant hierarchies involved in sport. As Celia Brackenridge and Anita White (1985) have shown, sport is owned, controlled and organized by white middle-class men. Sport can be redefined only if those involved in sport at this level begin this process of redefinition. Paul Willis (1982) reflects this position:

> A sport could be presented as a form of activity which emphasizes human similarity and not dissimilarity, a form of activity which expresses values which are indeed immeasurable, a form of activity which is concerned with individual well-being and satisfaction rather than with comparison. (Willis 1982: 14)

Within physical education it should be a priority to consider alternative forms of sport which, in the long term, will not only encourage different values but also encourage girls and boys, and eventually women and men, to enjoy sport on equal terms. This may mean that educators and those involved in sport need to develop new games and activities and take seriously sports such as handball and korfball (a cross between netball and basketball developed in Holland, with eight a side – four men and four women) as activities appropriate to both girls and boys. Although physical education is not synonymous with sport, sport remains the emphasis within the curriculum. This emphasis will remain, particularly if physical education continues to be identified as preparation for future leisure activities. If girls' physical education is not going to simply reinforce the gender divisions of leisure and sport in society then it must begin to question what it is preparing for and how it can begin the process of challenge and redefinition.

Physicality: muscles, strength and physical power

The research highlights the need to locate physicality and physical power relations as central to the analysis of gender relations. Therefore the development of individual potential in physical strength and power for girls must be a primary objective of girls' physical education. This requires effective challenges to the ideology of the physical, identified and discussed in this research, so that girls can develop confidence and assertiveness and, ultimately, greater control over their bodies. The most obvious recommendation is the inclusion of self-defence as an essential core element of teaching. Just as adult women are claiming the right to control and develop their own bodies for intrinsic satisfaction rather than sexual exploitation, so physical education must emphasize these values for young women. They must be encouraged to enjoy physical movement, to develop strength and muscular potential; to work together to discover body awareness and confidence. As Helen Lenskyj (1982) states, women tend to be alienated from their bodies and unaware of their physical potential. Girls' physical education should move away from stereotypical expectations of girls' physical potential and look to new directions which can motivate young women to be active, fit and physically developed. This might mean the development and introduction of 'new' sports and/or the development of new teaching approaches to the traditional games. The practical implications are difficult to determine and will require considerable action research in the schools.

The important issue remains the need for the fulfilment of physical potential and the awareness that muscular development, physical power and strength do not need to be the prerogative of men. The ideology of physicality is as powerful as the actual appropriation of muscle and strength by men. Girls and young women need to be encouraged to see the positive arguments concerning the development of physical strength and to challenge their construction as the passive recipients of male aggression and strength. 'Women fighting back' is an important slogan in the struggle to gain equality between the sexes. Part of this 'fight back' must be the realization that women too can be 'strong and resilient, capable of hard work and hard play' (Lenskyj 1982). As Helen Lenskyj argues, in a development of her work:

> Women's increasing participation in fitness-related activities, from dance exercise to body building, is potentially liberating. To feel at ease with one's body and to be aware of its strengths and weaknesses is to know oneself better. Moreover, the sense of achievement derived from physical fitness gains encourages women to tackle either physical or mental challenges. (Lenskyj 1986: 137)

Although girls' physical education remains locked within an emphasized femininity and the reinforcement of a 'feminine' physical potential it is also in a powerful position to challenge this crucial aspect of gender relations.

Consciousness-raising

In order to achieve the first four recommendations of this research, teachers, advisers and pupils need to develop an awareness of the significance of these issues. This implies that gender should be placed high on the agenda of initial teacher education courses, in-service courses, staff meetings and teacher – pupil discussion. From the evidence it is clear that the issue of gender is not a core component of the initial training of physical education teaching. However, this must become a priority if any of the recommendations of this research are to be implemented. Many of the women teachers currently in a position to initiate change were trained years ago and clearly retain gender-stereotyped attitudes. As Rosemary Deem (1986) emphasizes, in relation to policy implementation, teachers must admit first that there is a problem before they can or will question their practice. Pratt (1985) found that in general physical education teachers remain unsympathetic to the notion of equal opportunities between girls and boys in school. Yet teacher commitment is necessary for change to be implemented. It is vital, therefore, that gender is discussed and action initiated at advisory level, in teacher education and in in-service training. Initially the setting up of teacher support groups for those teachers with a personal commitment to anti-sexist strategies within physical education would be a positive move of support for those isolated at work in sceptical, and even hostile, environments. Within schools, physical education can contribute to the creation of a positive 'female' atmosphere by the use of photographs and displays in the teaching areas. The research found in many schools either a lack of display material or the inappropriate use of posters exhibiting typically male sporting 'heroes'. There should be positive images of women which challenge the stereotyped ideas of women in relation to appearance, body image, shape and dress and which encourage young women's participation in, and enjoyment of, physical activity.

Related to this is the need to promote active teacher – pupil discussion about the main issues of 'physicality' and 'sexuality'.

Adolescent young women require encouragement in addressing these issues within a broader political framework. If physical 'education' is to move beyond its rigid traditions then it must tackle directly issues contextualized within the politics of sexuality and the structure of gender divisions. This confirms the priority of situating physical education within broader structural relations not only theoretically but also at a practical level with the pupils. There must be an awareness that social relations outside the school (e.g. in the family) directly influence gender in the school. Pupils need to be aware and question who it is who supports their physical education by providing them with clean kit and, indeed, what the reality is and where the responsibility lies, for out-of-school and post-school sport and leisure opportunities for young women. These issues need to be addressed not only formally in physical education time but also constantly in the informal contacts between staff and pupils.

Future research

Finally, this research raises a number of issues which require future investigation.

Boys, masculinity and physical education

If gender divisions are to be challenged then there must be concern for the physical education of both girls and boys. There is a need for research which looks at the relationship between boys' physical education and the reinforcement, production and reproduction of hegemonic masculinity. If girls' physical education reproduces an ideology of the physical which constructs young women as physically subordinate to men then there is a need to consider the proposition that male physical education reproduces an ideology of the physical which underpins a culture of masculinity emphasizing strength, toughness, competitiveness and physical domination. Without identifying and challenging the dynamics of gender in the schooling of boys, male–female power relations cannot change.

Towards an analysis of race, class and gender

As discussed previously, there is a need for future research to concentrate on the relationship between race, class and gender within physical education. There is a lack of research into race and sport or leisure although race and schooling is a developing area. Future research into physical education should centre its analysis on an understanding of race, racism and physical education teaching.

Pupils' perceptions and expectations

There is a need for more in-depth cultural research which would provide analyses of pupils' perceptions and expectations about gender and physical education. At present the emphasis has been on teachers and it needs to shift to consider pupils' attitudes and ideas.

Initial training and in-service training

This area is recognized as of crucial importance for future policy initiatives. Future research needs to assess the impact of current debates about gender on both physical education initial and in-service courses. This research is necessary in order to identify the gaps and weaknesses in these areas, assess current projects, courses and initiatives relating to gender and point towards future directions.

Sport, leisure, family and the division of labour

More research concerned with the relationships between insititutions needs to develop in order to provide a fuller analysis of gender, race and class. Research, for example, which looks at the connections between the family and physical education experiences and teachings, the relationship between physical education and future leisure and sport activities.

Primary school physical education and gender

Throughout the research it became clear that the teaching of secondary school physical education is heavily dependent on the primary school curriculum. There needs to be in-depth qualitative research which questions both girls' and boys' experiences of physical education at primary school level, and a structural analysis of primary school physical education looking at the primary school curriculum and teaching in relation to gender, class and race.

The National Curriculum, gender and physical education

The 1990s is a time of considerable change in the structure of secondary schooling and research is necessary to consider the implications of the National Curriculum for the future physical education of both girls and boys. In particular, it will be important to monitor the

impact of the National Curriculum on equal opportunity policies
and initiatives (Flintoff 1990).

These are recommendations general to both short-term and long-
term reforms in the 'classroom' of physical education. Although the
implementation of 'reforms' is of value, however, in the long-term
physical education needs to question fundamental issues around
physicality and sexuality. For 'physical' power relations and, ultimately, the politics of patriarchy to be challenged, girls and young
women should be encouraged to enjoy physical movement on their
own terms and develop confidence, assertiveness and control over
their own bodies. Most importantly, gender relations cannot be
altered fundamentally by women alone. It is for men also to take up
the challenge, both in physical education and in wider society, for
any future radical restructuring of gender relations to take place.
However, this research demonstrates that feminist analyses of
schooling must always include a full consideration of the complex
relations between gender and physical education. Physical education *is* in a position to initiate change which could influence not
only those teachers and pupils directly involved in feminist innovations but also, in the long term, to a redefinition of gender.
There is a need for feminist analyses and approaches to physical
education in order to inform policy and contribute to a fuller understanding of gender relations in society. M. Ann Hall (1985) points
out that

> nowhere is there a recognition among feminist theorists/scholars as
> to the fact that sport plays a considerable role in the reproduction of a
> specifically patriarchal social order and could, therefore, be signi-
> ficant in the transformation of that order. At the very least it can
> provide a site of resistance. Let us get on with the analysis and histori-
> cal work necessary. By doing so we will be making an important
> contribution to some essential thinking about the sociology of
> sport – as well as to feminist theory. (Hall 1985: 40)

M. Ann Hall's concern for the sociology of sport needs to be
extended to a critical analysis of physical education. This research
has begun to address this issue by combining empirical investigation
and feminist theoretical analysis. For the future it is important that
critical work in physical education is maintained and extended to
ensure that not only girls and young women but also boys and young
men receive a *physical* education that is sensitive to, aware of and
prepared to challenge gender inequalities.

Appendix: Methodology

The research developed from a feminist standpoint which recognized women's oppression and identified the need to investigate an important aspect of young women's schooling in order to challenge gender inequalities and inform future policy decisions. It began from an awareness of gender power relations both in an institutional, structural form and in the practices of those who hold power, i.e. advisers, heads of departments, and so on. Studying the structures alone, however, does not necessarily reveal ideological positions. The aim was to examine structures and practices which might sustain or reproduce gender inequalities, together with the ideological underpinnings of this institutional form. The adoption of quantitative techniques, which reduce the analysis to a discussion of organizational 'facts', was considered inadequate and inappropriate given that critical feminist research aims to situate gender inequalities in broader structural and ideological contexts. While it is important to know what is taught to girls in their physical education lessons, how often they have curricular and extra-curricular activities, this restricts the identification of inequality to an overt level.

Further, it is necessary to look more deeply and qualitatively at the attitudes and ideas of those who are the decision-makers in the school physical education situation (advisers and heads of departments) and at their practices in the everyday situation of physical education teaching. Thus a case study approach was adopted which considered one local education authority in depth. A number of research techniques were used in order to obtain a full and complete 'picture' of girls' physical education throughout the LEA.

Library research

This provided informed historical and political contexts for the contemporary material. It involved searches of primary and secondary source material including educational documents and reports, original journals and autobiographical and biographical accounts of girls' schooling and physical education in secondary education.

Structured, open-ended interviews

Interviews were conducted with the physical education adviser, the heads of girls' physical education in all the secondary schools and the peripatetic staff who worked within the LEA. The interviews were taped using a small hand-held recorder, permission having been obtained prior to each interview. The interviews lasted between thirty minutes and eighty minutes and were conducted in school during the lunch-break, 'free' teaching period or immediately after school.

Case study observation

This aspect of the research aimed to assess how the stated policies and personal attitudes of the key personnel in physical education were articulated in practice. The everyday practices of physical education were observed with the opportunity to conduct more informal interviews and discussion with those involved in the teaching and organization of girls' physical education in selected schools.

Four schools were selected as representative of the types of schools available in the city, each offering contrasting and quite different emphases in their approach to, and practice of, physical education. Information gained from the first interviewing stage of the research informed this decision.

School	Type	Intake	Pupils
Heyfield	Co-educational inner city comprehensive	Multi-racial, working-class	1,400
Rosehill	Co-educational suburban comprehensive	Predominantly white, working-class and middle-class	1,400

Table continued

Townley	Single-sex inner city comprehensive	White, working-class	1,200 Girls
Archway	Single-sex Church of England comprehensive	Predominantly white, middle-class	750 Girls

Approximately half a term (six weeks) was spent full time in each of the case study schools (a total of two terms' participant observation). In each school, written information was collected on the stated policy and organization of both the school in general and physical education in particular. Daily observations were recorded in a field diary.

Thus the research did not use a 'feminist method' but was based on a feminist methodology which acknowledged the need for research on women and gender, was grounded in the experiences of the researched and researcher, developed out of a feminist consciousness and was subject to 'ongoing attempts to understand, explain, re-explain what is going on' (Stanley and Wise 1983: 161). Most importantly, throughout the research process there were continual interconnections made between theory, empirical research and political responses.

Bibliography

Acker, S., Megarry, J., Nisbet, S. and Hoyle, E. (1984) *World Yearbook of Education 1984: Women and Education*. London, Kogan Page.

Amos, V. and Parmar, P. (1984) Challenging imperial feminism, *Feminist Review*, 17: 3–20.

Archer, R. L. (1964) *Rousseau J. J., Emile, Julie and Other Writings*. New York.

Arnot, M. (1982) Educating girls. *Unit 13 Changing Experience of Women*. Milton Keynes, Open University Educational Enterprises.

Arnot, M. (1984) A feminist perspective on the relationship between family life and school life, *Boston University Journal of Education*, 166, March: 5–24.

Arnot, M. and Weiner, G. (eds) (1987) *Gender and the Politics of Schooling*. Milton Keynes, Open University Press.

Atkinson, P. (1978) Fitness, feminism and schooling. In S. Delamont and L. Duffin (eds) *The Nineteenth Century Woman: Her Cultural and Physical World*. London, Croom Helm.

Ball, S. (1987) *The Micro-Politics of the School*. London, Methuen.

Beechey, V. (1979) On patriarchy, *Feminist Review*, 1: 66–82.

Belotti, E. G. (1975) *Little Girls*. London, Writers and Readers Publishing Co-operative.

Beveridge Report (1942) *Report on the Social Insurance and Allied Services*, Cmd 6404. London, HMSO.

Beveridge, W. (1948) *Full Employment in a Free Society*, Cmd 7321. London, HMSO.

Birrel, S. (1984) Separatism as an issue in women's sport, *Arena Review*, 18, 2: 24–8.

Bjorksten, E. (1932) *Principles of Gymnastics for Women and Girls*. London.

Bland, L. (1984) The case of the Yorkshire Ripper: mad, bad, beast or male?

In P. Scraton and P. Gordon (eds) *Causes for Concern*. Harmondsworth, Penguin.

Board of Education Report (1936) *The Health of the School Child*. London, HMSO.

Boslooper, T. and Hayes, M. (1974) *The Femininity Game*. New York, Skein & Day.

Bowles, S. and Gintis, H. (1976) *Schooling in Capitalist America*. London, Routledge & Kegan Paul.

Brackenridge, C. and White, A. (1985) Who rules sport?*International Review of the Sociology of Sport*, 20, 1/2: 95–107.

British Medical Journal (1922) *The Physical Education of Girls*.

Brohm, J-M. (1976) *Sport: A Prison of Measured Time*. London, Ink Links.

Brownmillar, S. (1975) *Against Our Will: Men, Women and Rape*. New York, Simon & Schuster.

Bryan, B., Dadzie, S. and Scafe, S. (1985) *The Heart of the Race: Black Women's Lives in Britain*. London, Virago Press.

Burstall, S. (1907) *English High Schools for Girls: Their Aims, Organisation and Management*. New York, Longman.

Byrne, E. (1974) *Planning and Educational Inequality*. Slough, National Foundation for Educational Research.

Carby, H. V. (1982) White women listen! Black feminism and the boundaries of sisterhood. In Centre for Contemporary Cultural Studies (ed.) *The Empire Strikes Back*. London, Hutchinson.

Carrington, B. and Williams, T. (1988) Patriarchy and ethnicity: the link between school physical education and community leisure activities. In J. Evans (ed.) *Teachers, Teaching and Control in Physical Education*. Lewes, Falmer Press.

Carrington, B., Chivers, T. and Williams, T. (1987). Gender, leisure and sport: a case-study of young people of South Asian descent, *Leisure Studies*, 6: 265–79.

Clarricoates, K. (1986) The experience of patriarchal schooling, *Interchange*, 12, 2–3: 183–205.

Cockburn, C. (1981) The material of male power, *Feminist Review*, 9: 41–58.

Cockburn, C. (1983) *Brothers*. London, Pluto Press.

Connell, R.W. (1983) *Which Way is Up? Essays on Class, Sex and Culture*. Sydney, Allen & Unwin.

Connell, R.W. (1987) *Gender and Power*. Cambridge, Polity.

Coveney, L. et al. (1984) *The Sexuality Papers: Male Sexuality and the Social Control of Women*. London, Hutchinson.

Coward, R. (1984) *Female Desire: Women's Sexuality Today*. London, Paladin.

Crunden, C. (1974) *A History of Anstey College of Physical Education 1897–1972*. Anstey College of Physical Education, Birmingham.

David, M. (1980) *The State, the Family and Education*. London, Routledge & Kegan Paul.

De Beauvoir, S. (1974) *The Second Sex*. Harmondsworth, Penguin.

Deem, R. (1978) *Women and Schooling*. London, Routledge & Kegan Paul.

Deem, R. (ed.) (1980) *Schooling for Women's Work*. London, Routledge & Kegan Paul.

Deem, R. (1981) Social policy and education: towards a political economy of schooling and sexual divisions, *British Journal of Sociology of Education*, 2, 1: 3–12.

Deem, R. (1984) *Co-education Reconsidered*. Milton Keynes, Open University Press.

Deem, R. (1986). Bringing gender equality into schools. In S. Walker and J. Barton (eds) *Changing Policies, Changing Teachers*. Milton Keynes, Open University Press.

Delamont, S. (1980) *Sex Roles and the School*. London, Methuen.

Delphy, C. (1984) *Close to Home*. London, Hutchison.

DHSS (1985) *Social Trends*. London, HMSO.

Duffin, L. (1978) The conspicuous consumptive: woman as an invalid. In S. Delamont and L. Duffin (eds) *The Nineteenth Century Woman*. London, Croom Helm.

Dworkin, A. (1981) *Pornography: Men Possessing Women*. London, Pedigree.

Dyer, K. (1982) *Catching Up the Men: Women in Sport*. London, Junction Books.

Dyhouse, C. (1976) Social Darwinistic ideas and the development of women's education in England, 1880–1920, *History of Education*, 5, 1: 41–58.

Dyhouse, C. (1981) *Girls Growing Up in Late Victorian England*. London, Routledge & Kegan Paul.

Ehrenrich, B. and English, D. (1975) *Complaints and Disorders: The Sexual Politics of Sickness*. London, Writers and Readers Cooperative.

Eisenstein, H. (1984) *Contemporary Feminist Thought*. London, Counterpoint.

Eisenstein, Z. (1979) *Capitalist Patriarchy and the Case for Socialist Feminism*. London, Monthly Review Press.

Engels, F. (1968) *The Origin of the Family, Private Property and the State*. London, Lawrence & Wishart.

Evans, J. and Williams, T. (1988) Moving up and getting out: the classed and gendered career opportunities of physical education teachers. In J. Evans (ed.) *Teachers, Teaching and Control in Physical Education*. Lewes, Falmer Press.

Evans, J. et al. (1985) Some thoughts on the political implications of mixed sex grouping in the physical education curriculum. Paper presented to the *Sociology of Physical Education Conference*, Manchester University.

Fasting, K. and Pederston, K. (1987) The study of sport from the women's perspective. Paper presented at *Jyvaskyla Congress*, Finland.

Ferris, E. (1978) The myths surrounding women's participation in sport and exercise. *Report of the Langham Life 1st International Conference on Women and Sport*. London.

Firestone, S. (1971) *The Dialectic of Sex*. New York, Women's Press.

Flanagan (1985) New directions for physical education. Paper presented at the *1985 BAALPE Congress*, London.

Fletcher, S. (1984) *Women First: The Female Tradition in English Physical Education 1880–1980*. London, Athlone Press.

Flintoff, A. (1990) Physical education, equal opportunities and the National Curriculum: crisis or challenge, *PE Review*, 13, 2: 85–100.

Gold, R. (1954) Social field observations, *Social Forces*, autumn: 27–43.

Graydon, J. et al. (1985) Mixed physical education in the secondary school – an evaluation. Paper presented to *International Council for Health, PE and Recreation World Congress*.

Green, E., Hebron, S. and Woodward, D. (1987) *Women's Leisure in Sheffield*. London, ESRC/Sports Council.

Griffin, C. (1981) Young women and leisure: the transition from school to work. In A. Tomlinson (ed.) *Leisure and Social Control*. Brighton Polytechnic.

Griffin, C. (1985) *Typical Girls*. London, Routledge & Kegan Paul.

Hall, M.A. (1979) Intellectual sexism in physical education, unpublished article.

Hall, M.A. (1981) *Sport, Sex Roles and Sex Identity*. Ottawa, CRIAW Papers.

Hall, M.A. (1982) The player, the woman and the necessity of feminist scholarship, *1982 Proceedings of NAPEHE*. Ottawa.

Hall, M.A. (1984) Feminist prospects for the sociology of sport, *Arena Review*, 8: 26–34.

Hall, M.A. (1985) How should we theorize sport in a capitalist patriarchy? *International Review of Sociology of Sport*, 20: 109–15.

Hall, M.A. (1987) Masculinity as culture: the discourse of gender and sport. Paper presented to *Jyvaskyla Congress*, Finland.

Hall, S. (1982) Managing conflict, producing consent. *Unit 21, Block 5, D102 Social Sciences: A Foundation Course*. Milton Keynes, Open University Educational Enterprises.

Harding, S. (1988) *Feminism and Methodology*. Milton Keynes, Open University Press.

Hargreaves, J. (1986) *Sport, Power and Culture*. Cambridge, Polity Press.

Hargreaves, J.A. (1979) Playing like gentlemen while behaving like ladies, MA thesis, University of London.

Hargreaves, J.A. (ed.) (1982) *Sport, Culture and Ideology*. London, Routledge & Kegan Paul.

Hartmann, H. (1979) The unhappy marriage of marxism and feminism, *Capital and Class*, 8, summer.

Hoch, P. (1972) *Rip off the Big Game*. New York, Anchor.

Hooks, B. (1982) *Ain't I a Woman? Black Women and Feminism*. London, Pluto Press.

Hooks, B. (1989) *Talking Back. Thinking Feminist – Thinking Black*. Sheba.

Inner London Education Authority (ILEA) (1984) *Providing Equal Opportunities for Girls and Boys in Physical Education*. London, PE Teachers Centre.

Jackson, S. (1982) *Childhood and Sexuality*. Oxford, Basil Blackwell.

Jeffries, S. (1985) *The Spinster and her Enemies*. London, Pandora.

Journal of Scientific Physical Training (1918–19). vol. XI.

Journal of Scientific Physical Training (1919–20). vol. XII.

Journal of Scientific Physical Training (1926–7). vol. IX.

Kamm, J. (1958) *How Different From Us: Miss Buss and Miss Beale*. London, Bodley Head.

Kane, J. E. (1974) Physical Education in Schools. *Report of a Commission of Enquiry*. London, Physical Education Association of Great Britain and Northern Ireland.

Kenealy, A. (1920) *Feminism and Sex Extinction*. London.

Kristeva, J. (1982) *Desire in Language*. New York, Columbia University Press.

Lawrence, P. (1988) Games and athletics for secondary schools for girls, *Special Reports on Educational Subjects*, vol. 2. London, HMSO.

Leaman, O. (1984) *Sit on the Sidelines and Watch the Boys Play*. Harlow, Longman.

Lees, S. (1986) *Losing Out*. London, Hutchinson.

Lenskyj, H. (1982) I am strong, *University of Toronto, Women's News Magazine*, March–April: 13.

Lenskyj, H. (1986) *Out of Bounds: Women, Sport and Sexuality*. Toronto, Women's Press.

Llewellyn, M. (1980) Studying girls at school: the implications of confusion. In R. Deem (ed.) *Schooling for Women's Work*. London, Routledge & Kegan Paul.

Lovell, T. (1991) Sport, racism and young women. In G. Jarvie (ed.) *Sport, Racism and Ethnicity*. Lewes, Falmer Press.

McCrone, K. (1982) Victorian women and sport: the game in colleges and public schools, *Canadian Historical Association*, 1–39.

MacDonald, M. (1980) Socio-cultural reproduction and women's education. In R. Deem (ed.) *Schooling and Women's Work*. London, Routledge & Kegan Paul.

MacDonald, M. (1981) Schooling and the reproduction of class and gender relations. In R. Dale, G. Esland, R. Ferguson and M. MacDonald *Education and the State: Politics, Patriarchy and Practice*. Lewes, Falmer Press.

MacKinnon, C. (1982) Feminism, marxism, method and the state, *Signs*, 7, 3: 515–44.

McRobbie, A. (1978) Working class girls and the culture of femininity. In CCCS (ed.) *Women Take Issue*. London, Hutchinson.

Mahony, P. (1985) *Schools for the Boys?* London, Hutchinson.

Mangan, J.A. (1982) Social Darwinism, sport and English upper class education. Paper presented at conference on the *Social History of Nineteenth Century Sport*, Liverpool University.

May, J. (1969) *Madame Bergmann-Osterberg*. London, Harrop.

Measor, L. (1984) Sex education and adolescent sexuality, unpublished article.

Metheny, E. (1964) Sports and the feminine image, *Gymnasium*, 4.

Millet, K. (1971) *Sexual Politics*. New York, Equinox Books.

Mitchell, J. (1974) *Psychoanalysis and Feminism*. Harmondsworth, Pelican.

Murray, J.H. (1982) *Strong Minded Women*. Harmondsworth, Penguin.

Newsom, J. (1948) *The Education of Girls*. London, Faber & Faber.

Oakley, A. (1972) *Sex, Gender and Society*. London, Temple-Smith.

O'Brien, M. (1981) *The Politics of Reproduction*. London, Routledge & Kegan Paul.

Okeley, J. (1979) Privileged, schooled and finished: boarding education for girls. In S. Ardener (ed.) *Defining Females: The Nature of Women in Society*. London, Croom Helm.

Pantyazopoulou, E. (1979) The requirements of physical training and sport in female education, *Prospects*, IX, 4: 4–17.

Pratt, J. (1985) The attitudes of teachers. In J. Whyte, R. Deem, L. Kant and M. Cruikshank (eds) *Girl-Friendly Schooling*. London, Methuen.

Purvis, J. (1991) *A History of Women's Education in England*. Milton Keynes, Open University Press.

Rigauer, B. (1981) *Sport and Work*. New York, Columbia University Press.

Roberts, H. (ed.) (1981) *Doing Feminist Research*. London, Routledge & Kegan Paul.

Rosen, D. (1987) An outsider's view, *British Journal of Physical Education*, 17, 4: 152.

Rowbotham, S. (1973) *Hidden from History*. London, Pluto Press.

Schools Inquiry Commission (1868) *Royal Commission on School Education*. London.

Sharpe, S. (1976) *Just Like a Girl*. Harmondsworth, Penguin.

Sharpe, R. and Green, T. (1975) *Education and Social Control*. London, Routledge & Kegan Paul.

Smart, C. (1984) *The Ties That Bind*. London, Routledge & Kegan Paul.

Smith, D. (1977) *Feminism and Marxism: A Place to Begin, A Way to Go*. Vancouver, New Star Books.

Special Reports on Educational Subjects (1898) vol. 2. London, HMSO.

Spencer, H. (1861) *Education, Intellectual, Moral and Physical*. London.

Spender, D. (1982) *Invisible Women*. London, Writers and Readers Co-operative.

Spender, D. and Sarah, E. (eds) (1980) *Learning to Lose: Sexism and Education*. Women's Press.

Springhall, J. (1985) Rotten to the very core: leisure and youth 1830–1914, *Youth and Policy*, 14: 19–22.

Stanko, E. (1985) *Intimate Intrusions: Women's Experience of Male Violence*. London: Routledge.

Stanley, L. and Wise, S. (1983) *Breaking Out*. London, Routledge & Kegan Paul.

Stanworth, M. (1983) *Gender and Schooling*. London, Hutchinson.

Talbot, M. (1980) Women and sport: a leisure studies perspective, *Centre for Urban and Regional Studies Working Paper*, 77.

Therberge, N. (1984) On the need for a more adequate theory of sport participation, *Sociology of Sport*, 1: 17–32.

Walker, D. (1834) *Exercises for Ladies*. London.

Webb, I.M. (1967) Women's place in physical education in Great Britain 1800–1966, unpublished thesis, University of Leicester.

Weber, M. (1947) *The Theory of Social and Economic Organisations*. Glencoe Free Press.

Weedon, C. (1987) *Feminist Practice and Poststructuralist Theory*. Oxford, Basil Blackwell.

Weiner, G. (ed.) (1985) *Just a Bunch of Girls: Feminist Approaches to Schooling*. Milton Keynes, Open University Press.

Weiner, G. and Arnot, M. (1987) *Gender Under Scrutiny: New Inquiries in Education*. Hutchinson.

Weiss, P. (1969) *Sport – A Philosophical Inquiry*. London.

Williams, R. (1977) *Marxism and Literature*. New York, Oxford University Press.

Willis, P. (1974) *Performance and Meaning: A Socio-cultural View of Women in Sport*. Centre for Contemporary Cultural Studies, Birmingham.

Willis, P. (1982) Women in sport in ideology. In J. A. Hargreaves (ed.) *Sport, Culture and Ideology*. London, Routledge & Kegan Paul.

Wilson, E. (1980) *Only Half Way to Paradise*. London, Tavistock.

Wilson, E. (1981) *What is to be Done about Violence against Women?* Harmondsworth, Penguin.

Wimbush, E. and Talbot, M. (1988) *Relative Freedoms: Women and Leisure*. Milton Keynes, Open University Press.

Wolpe, A-M. (1977) *Some Processess in Sexist Education*. London, Women's Research and Resource Centre.

Young, I. (1980) Throwing like a girl, *Human Studies*, 3: 7–13.

Young, I. (1981) Beyond the unhappy marriage: a critique of the dual systems theory. In L. Sargent (ed.) *Women and Revolution*. Boston, Ma., South End Press.

Young, M. (1971) *Knowledge and Control*. London, Collier-MacMillan.

Index